Peggy Dymond Leavey

Peggy Dymond Leavey's ten previous books include *Sky Lake Summer*, *The Deep End Gang*, and *The Path Through the Trees*, all of which have been nominated for the Silver Birch Award. She has also been shortlisted for the Manitoba Young Readers' Choice award, the Arthur Ellis Award, and the Canadian Library Association Book of the Year for Children Award. Her most recent book, *Growing Up Ivy*, was published by Dundurn in 2010.

A retired librarian, Peggy has published stories and articles in newspapers and magazines and was contributing editor on three books of local history. Her interest in the pioneers of early motion pictures began with her research into the movie industry of her hometown, Trenton, Ontario — Canada's filmmaking capital from 1917–1934. Writing the life of Mary Pickford was a natural progression.

Visit Peggy at *www.peggydymondleavey.com*.

In the same collection

A QUEST BIOGRAPHY

MARY PICKFORD

CANADA'S SILENT SIREN, AMERICA'S SWEETHEART

Peggy Dymond Leavey

DUNDURN
TORONTO

Editor: Shannon Whibbs
Copy Editor: Matt Baker
Design: Jesse Hooper
Printer: Webcom

Library and Archives Canada Cataloguing in Publication

Leavey, Peggy Dymond
    Mary Pickford : Canada's silent siren, America's sweetheart / written by Peggy Dymond Leavey.

(A Quest biography)
Includes index.
Includes bibliographical references.
Issued also in electronic formats.
ISBN 978-1-55488-945-7

    1. Pickford, Mary, 1892-1979. 2. Motion picture actors and actresses--Canada--Biography. 3. Motion picture actors and actresses--United States--Biography. 4. Motion pictures--United States--History--20th century. I. Title. II. Series: Quest biography

PN2287.P5L43 2011   791.4302'8092   C2011-901907-8

1   2   3   4   5   15   14   13   12   11

 Conseil des Arts du Canada   Canada Council for the Arts   Canada    ONTARIO ARTS COUNCIL
CONSEIL DES ARTS DE L'ONTARIO

We acknowledge the support of the Canada Council for the Arts and the Ontario Arts Council for our publishing program. We also acknowledge the financial support of the Government of Canada through the Canada Book Fund and Livres Canada Books, and the Government of Ontario through the Ontario Book Publishing Tax Credit and the Ontario Media Development Corporation.

Care has been taken to trace the ownership of copyright material used in this book. The author and the publisher welcome any information enabling them to rectify any references or credits in subsequent editions.

                                                                        J. Kirk Howard, President

Printed and bound in Canada.
www.dundurn.com

        Dundurn   Gazelle Book Services Limited   Dundurn
3 Church Street, Suite 500   White Cross Mills   2250 Military Road
  Toronto, Ontario, Canada   High Town, Lancaster, England   Tonawanda, NY
        M5E 1M2   LA1 4XS   U.S.A. 14150

Adding sound to movies would be like adding lipstick to the Venus de Milo.

Mary Pickford

Contents

Acknowledgements

Twenty-two years ago, my first book told the story of the film-making industry that flourished before the days of talking pictures in the town where I lived. That was my first encounter with silent movies. I was delighted to discover, on reading Mary Pickford's filmography, that some of the same American actors who appeared in Mary's pictures had earlier travelled to Hollywood North to take roles in the silent movies made right here in Trenton, Ontario.

I am grateful to Michael Carroll, associate publisher and editorial director at Dundurn, for believing that I could write the life of Mary Pickford, Canada's "Golden Girl." My thanks to Matt Baker for his insightful editing, to John Thompson of Toronto's National Club for his assistance, to Helen Mason and Carolyn Moore, to the McArthur family for their technical skills, to my Toronto connections, Susan and Peter Butler, and to all who sent me clippings and showed interest in the project.

This book could not have been written without my having access to the many books available to me through the interlibrary loan system. I was also fortunate to be able to visit the first exhibition in the Canadian Film Gallery at the TIFF Bell Lightbox in Toronto, "Mary Pickford and the Invention of the Movie Star." It was a stunning collection.

Finally, a big thank you to my family, who put up with my total absorption in this project for so long. This book is for you.

Prologue

One morning, late in the year 1899, Charlotte Smith answered a knock at the front door of her Toronto home. Charlotte was a pretty woman in her mid-twenties, just five feet tall, with lustrous blue-black hair and a pleasantly rounded figure.

The stranger on the doorstep removed his hat. "I'm here about the room," he said.

Charlotte's three young children pressed around her, filling the doorway, eager to see who the caller might be. The little one, three-year old Jack (or Johnny, as he was known when he was on his best behaviour), and Lottie, who was five, had escaped the clutches of their older sister, Gladys.

Charlotte promptly lifted Johnny into Gladdie's arms and shooed them all back inside.

"The sign in your window, Madam? You have a room for rent?"

"Oh, I don't rent rooms to gentlemen, sir," Charlotte said. "I am a widow, you see. Except for little Johnny there, this is a household of women. I only ever take ladies as lodgers."

"But I am a married man," the stranger hastened to explain. "My wife will be with me in the city, wherever I stay. May I bring her around to meet you? You'll like her; I'm sure you will."

The man introduced himself as Mr. Murphy, and sensing that the young landlady seemed likely to reconsider his request, he suggested that he come back later for her answer.

Charlotte agreed and shut the door. Now there would be time to discuss the proposal with her invalid mother, Catherine Hennessey, who lived with her, and to confer with her sister Lizzie Watson, who lived next door to their Orde Street house.

In the end, the family agreed that renting the master bedroom under these circumstances was quite acceptable, and they voted in favour of the well-dressed gentleman.

It was impossible to know then, but by renting out the room to Mr. Murphy and his wife, Charlotte was setting in motion a series of events that would change the lives of the Smith family forever.

1

The Toronto Neighbourhood

Mary Pickford was born at 211 University Avenue, Toronto, shown centre.

Seven-year-old Gladys, so often in charge of her two younger siblings, had been born in a house on Toronto's University Avenue on April 8, 1892, the same year that the first electric streetcar went into service in the city and Queen's Park became the home of the provincial legislature.

Mary's birthplace, 211 University Avenue, was a tiny, two-storey brick row-house with only six rooms. There were no houses on the other side of the street, and out front the bridle path was shaded by flowering chestnuts and red maple trees.

Gladys later had pleasant memories of sailing like the wind down that path on her bicycle. And such was her attachment to her first home that when the house was torn down in 1943, she had twenty of its bricks sent to her in California.

But that was many years later, long after young Gladys Louise Smith had been dubbed "America's Sweetheart," and her name changed to Mary Pickford, known then as the highest paid woman in the world, now as the most powerful woman in the history of motion pictures.

Gladys's parents, John Charles Smith and Charlotte Hennessey, had both been born in Toronto, Charlotte possibly on Queen Street. John came from British Methodist stock. His father, Joseph Smith, had come to Canada from Liverpool, England, as an infant. John's mother was Sarah Key, who had been born in London and arrived in Canada when she was six years old. Sarah Key Smith would attend the same Methodist church in Toronto for the next eighty years and live to the age of ninety-one.

Charlotte's family were Irish Catholics. Her mother, Catherine Faeley, had come to Canada from Tralee, in County

Kerry in the south of Ireland. She had met John Pickford Hennessey, another immigrant from County Kerry, in Quebec.

Until she married John Smith, around 1890, young Charlotte Hennessey had been a devout Catholic, educated by the nuns at the convent school she attended in Toronto. Charlotte was living with her older sister, Lizzie, and Lizzie's husband, William Watson, when she first met John. Catherine Hennessey, the girls' mother, a widow since 1882, also shared their home.

In those days, Charlotte made her living as a seamstress, having learned the skill in the convent. After John and Charlotte married, they moved up the block from the Watsons, and Catherine Hennessey moved with them.

John Charles Smith was one of twelve children. He was a short man with a slight build. His eldest daughter, Gladys, would inherit his rippling, golden brown hair, his delicate hands. He was good-looking, funny, and although he was often described as a dreamer, everyone seemed to like John and wanted to help him. Unfortunately, he also had a fondness for "the drink."

John Charles could turn his hand to any type of work. He'd been a salesman, a farm worker, a cowboy, a stagehand, a bartender, and after marrying Charlotte, he had clerked at a candy and fruit counter in a fish shop. At the time of Gladys's birth, he was working as a printer.

Little Gladys adored her father, but she found his mother, Grandma Sarah Key Smith, quite formidable, as straitlaced as Queen Victoria, whom the young Gladys thought she resembled. The child remembered fleeing out of the way of dour Grandma Smith whenever the woman visited the house, garbed in her usual black dress and purple taffeta petticoats that rustled when she walked.

According to Gladys, one thing Grandma Smith could not stand was to see anyone enjoying themselves on the Sabbath.

"There was very little a family like ours *could* do on a Sunday," Mary Pickford later wrote in her memoir, *Sunshine and Shadow*. "Taking the beltway trolley that circled Toronto was about the only amusement. But that was enough for Grandma. For years she served on a citizens' committee to urge passage of a law against the operation of streetcars on the Sabbath."

When Gladys was about two, the family moved to a small house on Walton Street. Although the births of the two younger Smith children were never registered, Lottie, named Charlotte after her mother, was born sometime in June, 1893, and Johnny or Jack, probably in 1895.

Of her two parents, the young Gladys loved her father best. Her mother was always too busy to play with her, having three children to look after. For Charlotte, there was the endless washing, cooking, and sewing to do, as well as her own mother to care for.

But Gladys's more happy-go-lucky dad could always find the time to play. She used to love to walk up to Queen's Park with him and wander among the tulips, share a drink of ice-cold water from the copper cup that hung suspended on a chain at a fountain there, or go tobogganing in High Park.

Late in the 1890s, John Smith got hired on as a purser with Niagara Steamship Lines on one of the holiday paddle steamers that crossed Lake Ontario between Toronto and Lewiston, New York. One day, while working on the *Corona*, where he ran a candy counter, he bounded down the stairs to the lower deck and hit his head on a dangling iron pulley, causing a fatal blood clot in his brain. He died on February 11, 1898. His death certificate gives his age as thirty.

Although Mary Pickford never wrote of it in her memoirs, John Charles Smith, the good-natured dreamer, had skipped out on his young family three years before the accident. Ever since, Charlotte had referred to herself as a widow. It was considered more respectable to be widowed than abandoned, in Victorian times.

John may have come back home sometime after his injury, because he died in the house with his family nearby. Gladys remembered hearing her mother's screams the night he passed away. She recalled getting out of bed and going to look in the door of the room where her father lay — sleeping, she thought. Charlotte's hysterical screaming and pounding on the wall petrified the child, and it was her Aunt Lizzie who came and took Gladys away to comfort her.

Subsequently, the children were sent to live in various other households until Charlotte was able to bring her grief under control.

Sometime after John's death, the family moved farther up the block on Walton Street. They had gone through all their savings by the time John died. Nearly destitute, in spite of the collection the people in the neighbourhood had taken up for them, the family moved yet again to 9 Orde Street, next door to Lizzie. Charlotte managed to find work in a grocery store and took in sewing at night to try to provide for her family. Regardless, the neighbours occasionally had to step in with food for the children.

Gladys was old enough to remember her father as he was in happier times, and it was always with great affection. It had never been a secret that Lottie, Gladys's sister, who was younger than her by only fourteen months, had been John's favourite.

They'd all heard the story often enough: Money, already scarce, had been even more so by the time Lottie arrived in

1893, and Charlotte had bemoaned the fact that now there was another mouth to feed. Besides, she'd hoped this baby would be a boy. John was hurt by her disappointment. Never mind; from that day forward the young father would never let Lottie forget that one of her parents loved her. She was "Papa's own little baby. My Chuckie baby."

Gladys remembered how she and Lottie used to go to meet their father when he got off the streetcar each evening. Lottie was the one he'd scoop up in his arms, while Gladys, the little martyr, held back and waited for her father to come to her.

As a young child, Gladys's health was delicate, and she was often sick. She was frequently anemic, and at one time or another, she had been stricken with diphtheria, tuberculosis, pneumonia, as well as some undetermined nervous disorders. Because of Gladys's precarious health, Aunt Lizzie and Grandma Hennessey tended to spoil and pamper the child, which may have helped to ease any jealousy Gladys felt toward her younger sister.

After a visiting priest had one day discovered the household under quarantine, Gladys had been baptized Catholic and her middle name changed to Marie. Four-year-old Gladys had "black diphtheria," and the priest had feared for her young soul.

According to a later story, Charlotte never informed her husband of this hasty baptism, and after his death she had all three children baptized as Protestants, as a tribute to his memory.

Charlotte had taken Gladys a number of times over the years to consult with Dr. George B. Smith, the head of the children's hospital in Toronto. He and his wife were a wealthy, childless couple, and one day, well aware of the family's dire financial straits, Dr. Smith asked Charlotte if she would consider allowing him and his wife to adopt Gladys. He assured her that the child would be loved as their own and given all the material comforts Charlotte was unable to provide.

Charlotte refused at once. But when she later told her sister Lizzie about it, Lizzie criticized her for turning down the doctor's offer. Had Charlotte *really* been thinking about what was best for Gladys?

Sick at heart, Charlotte dressed her eldest child in her Sunday best and took her back to Dr. and Mrs. Smith's house for an interview. It was a large, comfortable home, and while they were there, the little girl was shown the bedroom that would be hers should she decide to stay.

"You can have anything you want, Gladys," the couple promised.

"Can I have a pony and cart? And chicken and ice cream every day?"

"Most certainly," was the answer.

Charlotte said nothing; the choice was going to be up to Gladys to make.

Later, waiting with her mother for the streetcar, the child chattered on about how thrilled Jack and Lottie were going to be about that pony and cart, how she would share the chicken and ice cream with her mother and Grandma Hennessey. That was when she learned her brother and sister were not going to be there to share in the doctor's largess. Gladys would no longer be part of their family, Charlotte explained. She would be Dr. and Mrs. Smith's little girl.

Gladys burst into tears at the prospect, and throwing her arms about her mother's neck, begged to be taken home.

"That's the end of that then," Charlotte declared. "There will be no more of that nonsense." And she vowed to tell Lizzie a thing or two when they got back.

Mary Pickford later acknowledged that that was the day when she became determined to take her beloved father's place in the family. She would be the one to keep them from ever breaking up. Gladys would be a child no longer. Instead, she became her mother's little helper, more a contemporary than a daughter, and as her love for her mother grew deeper, so too did the fear that she would one day lose her.

For a few months one winter, Gladys and Lottie attended the Louisa Street School in Toronto, where their father and all his brothers and sisters had gone. Because Charlotte had to be up and off to work by the time the little girls got themselves washed, dressed, and out the door in the morning, they were often late for classes.

One day, the principal, Miss Adams, fed up with their tardiness, threatened to punish the girls the next time they were late. She scared them half out of their wits with a story of a big black wagon, sent by the devil, which would come to collect them, and how they'd never see their mother again.

In terror, the two children ran out of the school into the subzero weather, without even putting their coats and leggings back on. When they tumbled, wide-eyed and out of breath, into the house again, they found their mother was there, having returned for something she'd forgotten. After hearing what had happened, Charlotte, who was silently seething, got the two dressed and marched them back to the school.

Miss Adams did not deny that she'd told the story to frighten the children, but she defended herself by saying that what they *really* needed was a good, sound thrashing.

Charlotte informed Miss Adams that if ever she laid a hand

on either child, Charlotte would go to the school board and lodge a complaint against her.

For weeks after the incident, Gladys had nightmares, waking in the night, screaming about the big black wagon. She stopped eating, and eventually the doctor advised Charlotte to take her out of school altogether. She was so often sick that she was frequently absent anyway. Later, Charlotte bought some text books, and wherever they happened to be, taught the three children their lessons herself. She had had the benefit of a good education at the convent when she was growing up.

When she was young, Gladys preferred playing with dolls to engaging in sports. But she loved to ride a bicycle, and if ever she saved up ten cents, she would rent a bike for a whole hour.

On Gladys's eighth birthday, Charlotte surprised her with a bicycle of her own. The child couldn't imagine how hard her mother was going to have to work to pay for such an extravagance. Appalled by the $25 price tag, the little girl at first refused to accept the present.

Gladys was coasting down University Avenue on her bicycle one day (there was just enough of a downhill slope that she didn't have to peddle), when she turned west onto Queen Street, right into the path of a pair of horses. She stood hard on the brakes, trying to avoid a collision, and was thrown off the bike, gouging her ankle. Although she carried the scar from the accident for many years, bike riding in the Toronto streets remained a happy memory she cherished for a lifetime. "Those were the moments," she wrote, "almost the only ones, when I was really a little girl."

On a visit to Toronto many years later, Mary Pickford had told reporters how she used to love to ride her bike in the city when she was a child. When she was driven over to be photographed in front of her former home, there, to her delight, sat a bicycle.

As young Gladys and her mother grew closer, Lottie and Jack banded together against their older sister. Even Charlotte would tease, tickle, and roughhouse on the floor at times with the younger two, jumping to her feet if Gladys entered the room, as if she'd been caught doing something she shouldn't.

That kind of reaction only served to reinforce the idea that Gladys was a spoilsport, someone who disapproved of anything that was fun, and Lottie and Jack retaliated by leaving her out of their games.

Committed now to being the father in the family, Gladys took the task of bringing up Lottie and Jack very seriously. It was a responsibility she felt for the rest of her siblings' too-short lives.

It is doubtful that Charlotte Smith had been aware of the occupation of the man to whom she agreed to rent the master bedroom in the Orde Street house, married or not. Mr. Murphy was the stage manager for the Cummings Stock Company, currently a tenant of the Princess Theatre on King Street in Toronto.

Theatres, at the end of the nineteenth century, had a reputation for being rowdy places, and Charlotte shared with many the puritanical view that theatre people, too, were not quite respectable.

Under the management of Ambrose Small, actor Robert Cummings had formed the Cummings Stock Company in 1897, the first stock company to be formed in Toronto since the 1870s. The company had rented the Princess Theatre for a season. Now, the stage manager was looking for a couple of children to take part in a schoolroom scene in *The Silver King*, a melodramatic play written by English dramatist Henry Arthur Jones and Henry Herman in 1882.

Melodramas, stage plays which Mary later described as both "dreadful" and "rip-roaring," were primarily aimed at working-class audiences. These entertainments could usually be counted on to deliver the requisite wicked landlord, agonized heroine, spectacular stage effects, and plenty of opportunity for the audience to hiss at the villain.

"We're putting on a play next week," Mr. Murphy explained to Charlotte, after he had settled himself into her spare room. "Would you consider letting your two little girls appear in the scene?" He went so far as to suggest that putting the children on the stage could make things a little easier for the Smith family, financially.

Charlotte was highly indignant. "I'm sorry," she said, "but I will never allow my innocent babies to associate with actresses who smoke."

"Oh, but the people in this group," Mr. Murphy assured her, "are a happy, respectable lot. They've been together for a long time." All he asked was for Charlotte to come backstage that night and see for herself that actors were good people.

Charlotte wrestled with the idea. The theatre was not far away, and it *would* be for only one week. The extra money the venture would provide was tempting.

With its two balconies and its private boxes on either side above the stage, the Princess Theatre was quite grand. Besides being the first public building in Toronto to be equipped with electric lights, the theatre could seat more than 1,500 people.

Charlotte made her visit backstage. Whatever she witnessed that night must have met with her approval. When the play opened on January 8, 1900, Lottie and Gladys Smith made their theatrical debuts. And Charlotte herself was recruited to play the organ in the wings. Among those in the audience on opening night was a contingent of Canadian soldiers, about to ship out to the Boer War in South Africa.

Gladys played two roles in the play. In the first act, she was a child referred to simply as "Big Girl." The part called for Big Girl to be mean to Cissy Denver, the daughter of the Silver King. Gladys had only one line: "Don't speak to her, girls; her father killed a man!" Lottie had a non-speaking role in this same schoolroom scene.

In the second act, Gladys played Cissy's brother, Ned — a part with no lines. All she was required to do was sit on the floor in the background and play quietly with a set of wooden blocks while the parents in the scene carried on a conversation at centre stage.

Gladys, however, became creative and built the blocks into a pyramid. Then she ran a toy horse into them, bringing them all crashing down. The noise startled "the Denvers," and the look on their faces at Gladys's bit of improvisation caused the biggest laugh of the night.

When the curtain closed, the stage manager had a stern warning for young Gladys: "You must never draw attention away from the main action. Do you realize you spoiled the speeches of the Silver King and his wife? You are never again to steal a scene." But he did let Gladys keep her "little piece of business" in the show.

Although *The Silver King* closed earlier than expected, it ran for six evening performances and two matinees. The girls each earned $10, which they turned over to Charlotte. Maybe the theatre wasn't so bad, after all.

When the Cummings Stock Company moved on, Gladys was hired for a variety show at Shea's, a Toronto vaudeville house. She got a part in a playlet, a one-act play, called *The Littlest Girl.*

It was a small role, with no lines. In fact, she was carried onto the stage, a tiny, sleeping child, and was passed from the arms of one actor to the lap of another. She was billed as "Baby Gladys Smith." She had just turned eight. Already, the little actress was feeling the love of the audience.

A nine-year-old song-and-dance girl named Elsie Janis was performing another act in the same variety show. Charlotte was already on the way to becoming a stage mother, a driving force behind her daughter's career, when she heard what the other child was being paid: somewhere between $55 and $75 per week. She asked Mrs. Janis how to go about preparing Gladys for such a brilliant career.

"Take her to see the finest plays and actors," Mrs. Janis advised. Although she added that Gladys must never imitate anyone else: "... first and above all, let her be herself."

In November 1900, Charlotte heard that the Valentine Stock Company, a much superior troupe, had moved into the Princess Theatre and was holding auditions for its production of *The Silver King.* She took Gladys over to apply — why shouldn't the child play the same two roles she'd had in the earlier production?

Gladys had other ideas for herself. She told Miss Anne Blanke, the head of the company, that she wanted to play Cissy Denver, a much larger role, but one that would allow her to be close to Jack Webster, the actor who played Cissy's father.

"That was all in the back of my head when I asked for the part of Cissy Denver," Mary Pickford wrote later. "Webster was to be my father in the play."

Following Mrs. Janis's advice, Gladys had been to the matinees of the Valentine Stock Company with her mother, or Aunt Lizzie and her cousins, sitting on their laps in order to see over the heads of the people in front and to save the price of another ticket. Jack

Webster was a member of the troupe, and little Gladys, without a father of her own, had become fixated on him.

But Charlotte was certain that Gladys would never be able to learn all the lines for the role of Cissy. Why, the child couldn't even read yet.

"Please, lady," Gladys begged, looking up into Miss Blanke's eyes. "Won't you let me try?" That heartfelt plea was enough for Charlotte, and mother and daughter left the theatre with the script in hand.

While they waited for the streetcar, under the light from the lamp post, Charlotte began to read Gladys her lines and the cues that she would need, and Gladys repeated them. She was determined she would learn the part, and by the time she went to bed that night she had already memorized the entire first act.

When *The Silver King* closed on November 24, 1900, Gladys Smith had become the Valentine Stock Company's official child actress. As was the custom, the company gave out souvenir buttons with her name on them. Gladys had discovered that she loved the theatre, enjoyed being the centre of attention. And all the other actors adored this tiny, beautiful child with the expressive, hazel eyes and the head of golden curls.

Still with the Valentine Stock Company, on January 21, 1901, Gladys played the title role in *Bootle's Baby*, a comedy and another opportunity to be on the stage with Jack Webster, her substitute father. Unfortunately, the production ran the same week as the death of Queen Victoria, and as a result, the theatre audience was sparse.

Between February and May of that year, the Valentine Stock Company presented several plays for their Toronto audiences, including *At the Little Red Schoolhouse* by Hal Reid, an American author of melodramas. Gladys got the role of Mabel Payne in the production, and Lottie and Jack both had small roles. Charlotte, too, was hired, as an understudy. The play opened April 1, 1901, at the Princess Theatre.

Gladys's next role was as little Eva, "a saintly child," in a play based on Harriet Beecher Stowe's book *Uncle Tom's Cabin*. It was the most popular play in U.S. history, and had one of the most famous death scenes in theatre. It opened in Toronto on April 8, 1901, on Gladys's ninth birthday. Her last appearance with the Valentine Stock Company was as little Willy, in the play *East Lynne*, in May 1901.

The author of *At the Little Red Schoolhouse*, Hal Reid, had come to Toronto to supervise his play's production. He was impressed with the enthusiastic response of the audiences and promised to cast the Smiths in a production of the play, which was to tour in the U.S. that fall. It would open on Broadway, and the family would have to be prepared to move to New York.

On the strength of that promise, Charlotte sold the family's furniture, and they all made ready for the move. Charlotte threw herself wholeheartedly into her role as Gladys's drama coach, teaching her how to enunciate each word clearly and project her voice to the man sitting in the back row of the theatre.

She urged Gladys to forget all the dramatic gestures. "If you *feel* something very deeply," Charlotte said, "your arms, your legs, every part of your being will respond to that thought." It was advice the girl would remember for the rest of her acting life.

In addition to absorbing these teachings from her mother, Gladys learned life lessons from the very melodramas in which she played, lessons which she took quite seriously — heroines gained dignity through their own suffering, and if you worked hard enough, nothing could stand in your way.

And work young Gladys did.

2

Nineteen Weeks of One-Night Stands

Waiting at home in Toronto for the call to Broadway, the Smith family was unaware that Hal Reid had sold the producing rights to *At the Little Red Schoolhouse* and forgotten about his commitment to them.

The play, now revised and renamed *In Convict Stripes*, went on the road in September 1901 without them. Gladys's role as Mabel Payne had been filled by another child actress, Lillian Gish, from Springfield, Ohio.

When the touring company reached Buffalo in late fall, Lillian's chaperone, a friend of her mother's, became ill and was forced to return to New York City for an operation. This turn of events forced Lillian to resign, and, fortunately, someone in the cast remembered Gladys Smith. A wire went out to Charlotte in Toronto: "We want Gladys. Only Gladys."

Charlotte's terse reply was that if they wanted one member of the family, they had to take them all.

The company came up with jobs for everyone. Gladys played her previous role of Mabel Payne, Charlotte understudied all the female adult roles, Lottie understudied the role she'd played in Toronto — Johnny Watson, Mabel's little boyfriend — and both Lottie and Jack were walk-ons in a schoolhouse scene.

The pay was a grand total of $20 a week. Somehow, over the season, the family managed to put together enough money to buy the most prized possession of any professional actor at the time: a theatrical trunk. There was no turning back now.

The Smiths travelled from Buffalo to New York City while they were doing one-night stands with *In Convict Stripes*. Because many of the touring shows were being cast in New York, Charlotte was anxious to see what work there might be for the family for the next season. New York City was the mecca for actors, offering better quality shows and more refined audiences. The word was that even the food would be better in New York City.

Now the four Smiths began a familiar pattern, one that would repeat itself many times over the ensuing years. They joined the mind-numbing and ultimately discouraging job hunt, pounding the pavement with hundreds of other out-of-work actors who made the rounds of the casting offices.

"The picture of Mother, Lottie, Jack, and me trudging along to these offices will stay with me to my dying day," Mary wrote, years later.

The theatrical boarding houses in New York City were all jammed with hopefuls. When the Smith family arrived in the 1901–02 season, there were 314 plays running in the city. That number doubled if you counted all the productions touring the U.S. and Canada. Even the smallest town — and they all had at least one theatre — could host 200 one-night stands in a single year.

For the next six years, the Smith family (sometimes together, sometimes only one or two of them) travelled the rails in touring productions that covered the United States and occasionally went north into Canada.

Between engagements, the family would often live in New York City in order to be close to the casting offices. Underpaid and frequently hungry, they lived in boarding houses, dreary tenement flats, or fleabag hotels where the dingy bathroom was at the end of the hall, and you had to pay for the privilege of using the tub.

From time to time, the family lived in a fifth floor walk-up with two seamstress friends, "Aunties" Kate and Minnie Whelan. One summer they shared an apartment in Manhattan with the Gish family, consisting of Mary Gish and her two actress daughters, Lillian and Dorothy — another family of barnstorming actors. The Gish sisters and Mary Pickford often appeared in different productions of the same plays over the years.

Barnstorming in road shows meant the Smiths often had to run, almost as soon as the final curtain fell, to catch a train for the next town. They couldn't afford a berth and spent the nights sitting up, huddled together for warmth on the hard seats of the train.

Mary, age nine, as she appeared in 1901 for Uncle Tom's Cabin. *She was playing the role of Little Eva.*

If they stayed overnight in a dollar hotel, they would have to get up in the chill of early morning to catch the milk train, one that stopped at every little dot on the map. Only the threat of being left behind would get little Jack out of bed to board the train in the dark. Breakfast might be stale sandwiches left over from the day before, washed down with a drink of water.

Gladys learned to literally sleep on her feet. Years later, it wasn't uncommon to see her snatching a quick nap on the set, standing upright, with her back against the wall.

From the small salaries the actors earned on tour, they had to pay all their expenses on the road and provide their own costumes. They did their laundry at night, heating the wash water any way they could.

For the most part, the plays in which the Smiths appeared were melodramas, part of the "ten-twent'-thirt's" circuit, so-called because the price of admission was between ten and thirty cents. By comparison, Broadway theatres were charging $2.50 for their best seats.

The audiences were often boisterous or rude, but young Gladys had developed her own technique for getting their attention. She would stop dead and refuse to continue, turning her back on the people in the seats and glaring at them over her determined little shoulder. That usually worked. At ten, she was a tiny, ethereal beauty, her golden hair worn in long ringlets. Lottie, too, was a pretty child, with dark, wide-set eyes and a generous mouth. But Lottie's beauty would not cause heads to turn, the way Gladys's did.

In New York, Charlotte finally found work for the whole family in *The Fatal Wedding*, a hit play by Theodore Kraemer. Since work on the play would not begin until the fall, the Smiths returned to Toronto for the summer. With their funds almost gone, they lived in rented rooms in a house in the city.

Just before it was time to set out again to start rehearsals in New York, Charlotte became sick. She needed to have surgery. Because the family couldn't afford a hospital, the operation was performed right there, in the rooming house.

Twenty-four hours later, they were all back on the train, heading for New York City. Years afterward, Mary Pickford marvelled at how her mother, still in pain, had survived that overnight journey.

They arrived in New York City just in time to get to rehearsal. None of them had eaten anything since the day before, and the director wouldn't even allow the children a minute to get Charlotte a cup of tea.

The first performance of *The Fatal Wedding* in 1903 was a one-night stand in Pottsville, Pennsylvania. Brightly coloured handbills, proclaiming, "Baby Gladys Smith is a Wonder," were plastered all around the town. Lottie had been hired to understudy her sister's role, and Jack was an extra.

Charlotte was playing an Irish cook in the play. Other than being an understudy, it was her first theatrical role. In order to get the part, she had lied and told the director that she was experienced. Charlotte had the opening lines in the play, and backstage, the three children held their breaths and prayed that their mother would be able to remember them.

"Mother had real talent," Mary said in an interview, years later. "More than I ever imagined she'd have. And she could mimic almost any accent."

From Pottsville, the tour continued its route in a southerly direction. That season, the Smith family endured nineteen weeks of one-night stands, with eight or nine performances per week, including matinees. Every day meant a different town.

The tours always finished their season by late spring, and there would be a break before they started up again in the fall.

One summer, while the Smiths and the Gishes were living together in New York, Mary Gish opened a candy stand on the grounds of the Fort George amusement park. In the morning, both families would ride the streetcar to the site, where they'd help to pop the corn, put it into bags, and wrap candies. At lunchtime the youngsters would visit another stand that sold fried potatoes, enjoying a hot lunch for a nickel. In the evenings, Charlotte and Mary Gish sewed costumes for the coming season.

Even Mrs. Gish acknowledged Gladys's keen financial sense, and it was Gladys who prepared the budget for the little group, figuring out how much money they could spend on food. She was also responsible for keeping an eye on the younger children when their mothers were out looking for work for everyone.

The children didn't have to worry about being entertained, because Gladys had become quite skilled at getting them into the theatres to see any play that was worth seeing. The young entrepreneur would present a card at the stage door that read, "Gladys Smith. Little Red Schoolhouse Company." Boldly, she'd ask the theatre manager if he recognized fellow professionals. Unless the place was sold out, and as long as the manager was feeling generous, the children would be allowed to climb up to the gallery to watch the performance.

"Watch and learn," Gladys would instruct the other youngsters, with authority. "Maybe someday *we'll* play on Broadway." Being the eldest of the group, Gladys was looked up to by the Gish sisters, if not by her own siblings.

Occasionally during those touring years, the Smiths would return to Toronto for the summer, and they were there in 1904, the year Grandma Hennessey died. Whenever they were in the city, Gladys would take Lottie and Jack around to the stage door of the Princess, the Majestic, and the Grand Theatres, trying to get small parts in order to bring in some money during the off season. It was always difficult to find work for everyone.

Gladys and Lottie toured for eleven weeks in *The Child Wife*, in the 1904–1905 season, and Jack and Charlotte stayed in New York, where Charlotte kept looking for work. She'd made arrangements for a married couple in the touring company to keep an eye on her girls while they were on the road. Instead, the actors/chaperones, whom Gladys decided didn't like children, did everything possible to avoid them.

By the time the tour reached Baltimore, Gladys had decided to take matters into her own hands. She and Lottie ditched the couple, jumped off the streetcar in which the others were travelling, at three in the morning, and found their own accommodations in a downtown hotel.

Gladys's salary during the run was $25 a week. Every payday she would change each five dollar bill into five one-dollar bills — to make it look like more — and the girls would carry the cash in chamois "boodlebags" that they wore around their necks.

By Christmas time, she and Lottie had accumulated $68, but they worried now about carrying around that amount of cash, especially since their room in the Baltimore hotel was above the saloon. Alone together on Christmas Day, perhaps as a way to pass the time, they hid the money in various places throughout their hotel room, only to later change their minds and hide it someplace else. The following morning they took the boodle-bags to the post office and sent Charlotte a money order for the full amount.

In 1905 Gladys played the part of Freckles in *The Gypsy Girl*, another play by Hal Reid. This time she earned $40 a week and sent fifteen back to Charlotte, who was living in Brooklyn with the younger two.

In September of that same year, Charlotte was fortunate to find work for the whole family again, in Chauncey Olcott's production of *Edmund Burke*, an Irish musical. Olcott, an actor and producer and the star of the show, was looking for three children for his production: two big boys and a small girl — the opposite of what the Smiths could provide. Charlotte was quick to assure the man that her three children could play both boys and girls with ease.

Gladys and Lottie were given the boys' roles, and Jack, much to his disgust, played Lady Edith. Before each performance, Gladys would have to coax and beg her little brother into donning the wig, the voluminous petticoats, the satin dress, and the long pantalets he was to wear for his role.

"Jack would finally give in," Mary later wrote, "but to show his defiance, the minute he got off stage he would lift his skirts right up over his head as he climbed the stairs to the dressing room and show off his long pantalets."

The family was proud of what it had achieved, having risen from third-rate stock companies to playing in a Chauncey Olcott production in only five years. By way of reward, the Smiths decided that, for the run of the play, they would adopt for themselves the dignified middle name of "Millbourne."

Edmund Burke opened at Brooklyn's Majestic Theatre on November 2, 1905, and the engagement lasted until May 1906. "The three Smith youngsters ... made a clever trio of children for Mr. Olcott, and their work was most praiseworthy," read the *New York Clipper* in a review on October 7, 1905, prior to the official opening.

When the play closed, Jack and Lottie went back to Toronto to stay with Aunt Lizzie, while Charlotte accompanied Gladys in a tour of *Wedded with No Wife*.

A year later, Gladys signed on to play another boy's role, this time in *For a Human Life*, a Hal Reid melodrama. In her role as Patsy Poore, Gladys had to wear a bright red wig over her long hair. Charlotte had threatened to walk out, with her daughter in tow, when the stage manager had suggested that Gladys's blonde curls be cut off. Absolutely not! But, with so much of her own hair to hide under the wig, Gladys went on stage feeling as if her head was the size of a large pot.

During the 1907 road tour of *For a Human Life*, she was chaperoned by Jean Patriquin, an older actress who played the villainess in the production. Miss Patriquin willingly became Gladys's school tutor, poring over the textbooks the girl took on tour and helping her to obtain some newer and better ones.

Mary Pickford always maintained that she had learned to read from watching the billboards and signs from the windows of the train, and that she learned to spell "Schenectady" while waiting on the station platform.

This tour was booked into a much poorer quality of theatre; the audiences were filled with boorish types who hooted and jeered the players. Gladys hated it. But she believed that it was her job to entertain, to make the audience laugh, to provide them with a little bit of joy. An audience, she felt, should never know of the fatigue and disappointment the actors were suffering.

Gladys was living in squalor, feeling exhausted and a little desperate. For the first time, she noticed the bleak look on the faces of some of the company's older actors, who were worn down from years spent in this difficult life. She told herself that, at the end of stock season, she'd go back to New York and try to get a part in a Broadway production. It was either that or get out of theatre altogether.

This life on the road was too hard on her family, Gladys decided. There was no time to rest or have any fun, and the only friends the two younger children had were the other members of the company. Whatever happened next would be up to Gladys. Despite the fact that Charlotte demanded loyalty and that her word was law, Gladys was as determined as ever to look out for all of them. So, when *For a Human Life* closed in Brooklyn, on May 18, 1907, and the rest of the family returned to Toronto, Gladys stayed behind in New York.

Just in case she failed to land on Broadway — and it had to be with one of the leading producers when it happened — she set about making plans for an alternative life for herself. She would become a clothes designer.

After some inquiries about entry-level jobs in the garment industry, she learned she could earn $5 a week pulling out basting threads. And she could always sell subscriptions to *Ladies' Home Journal*.

Gladys would live with the seamstress "aunties," and with whatever pittance she earned, she would go to night school and learn design. She was already quite good at drawing. Eventually, she might even open her own dressmaking parlour. For all of this, she was only fifteen at the time.

In exchange for living rent-free, Gladys kept house for the Whelans in their tiny New York tenement flat. At night, she slept in their Morris chair, her arms above her head, her feet on another chair, and dreamed big dreams of Broadway.

3

Broadway or Bust

Gladys Smith's assault on the Broadway casting offices began at the top, with David Belasco — a playwright and, after twenty-five years in the business, a top producer on Broadway. This native of San Francisco was so well-respected in his field that he was referred to as "the Maestro."

David Belasco held open auditions on Monday mornings. Throughout the summer of 1907, week after week, Gladys Smith showed up every Monday morning. And every Monday morning she, like hundreds of others, would be told, "Nothing today, thank you. Come back next week."

She began sending Belasco a barrage of letters, enclosing photographs of herself, each showing a different facial expression.

Finally, she decided she would not wait until the following Monday, and she marched into the building and right up the stairs to the door of Belasco's office. She thought that if she didn't find the great man himself, there was a chance that she'd run into

Blanche Bates, the actress who was appearing in his production of *The Girl of the Golden West*, and that perhaps Blanche would put in a good word for her.

There was a small setback in her plan, however, and Gladys was waylaid by the office boy. He refused to allow her to go any farther, and an argument ensued. Out in the hall, the tone of her voice grew so insistent that William Dean, Belasco's assistant, appeared to determine the cause. When he inquired as to why she was there, she replied, "My life depends on seeing Mr. Belasco!"

Her timing was perfect, because the Maestro was casting a civil war drama, *The Warrens of Virginia*, and just happened to be looking for a girl to play Betty Warren, a twelve-year-old. William Dean told Belasco about the persistent young girl with the long, golden curls.

When at last Gladys got to meet the great Belasco, the man looked down at the small, slender teen and asked, "You want to become an actress?"

"I am already an actress," Gladys replied. "But now I want to become a *good* one."

David Belasco agreed to give her an audition the following evening, and "Auntie" Minnie Whelan accompanied her to the theatre.

For her audition, Gladys played her Patsy Poore role from *For a Human Life*. She hoped Mr. Belasco would understand that the lines were from a very melodramatic play. The only prop she asked for was a kitchen chair, which was to represent a policeman.

When it was over, Belasco suggested that she work on perfecting her Southern accent. Gladys knew then that she had the part.

The Warrens of Virginia was a new drama by William DeMille. His younger brother, Cecil B. DeMille, was also in the cast and would be playing Gladys's older brother. She would be paid $25 a week for the season.

But first, Belasco decided, there was the little matter of her name. They had to find something less flat, he suggested, less mundane than Gladys Smith. "Gladys Louise Millbourne Smith," Gladys told him. Together, the two of them went over some of the other names in her family, finally settling on that of her maternal grandfather, John Pickford Hennessey.

"Pickford it is, then," Belasco said. "Is Gladys your only name? Haven't you another?"

After telling him that she'd been baptized Marie, Belasco suggested they exchange that for Mary.

All that was left now was to break the news to Charlotte, back in Toronto. Gladys hadn't told her mother about her earlier decision, about how she'd made up her mind that she

Pickford circa 1907, in The Warrens of Virginia.

would appear in a Broadway play that summer or give up the theatre forever. She knew how hard it would be to ever get Charlotte's approval for her night school/dress designer idea.

Late that same night, she sat down and wrote a letter to her mother. It was only two lines in length, written in big, black letters, like the headlines in a newspaper:

GLADYS SMITH NOW MARY PICKFORD ENGAGED BY DAVID BELASCO TO APPEAR ON BROADWAY THIS FALL.

David Belasco was a short, stocky man with a magnificent head of silver hair, one lock of which always fell over his forehead. Although Jewish, he liked to wear a clerical collar as part of his otherwise dark clothing.

"To me, David Belasco was like the King of England, Julius Caesar and Napoleon all rolled into one," Mary wrote. And Belasco realized that Mary's love for the theatre nearly matched his own. She was always the first to arrive at rehearsals, he noted, and the last to leave.

Belasco's theatrical productions were famous for their realistic settings, and the man insisted that every prop appearing on stage must be authentic. The company often worked late into the evening, and one night, when Mary was half asleep, sitting in a stage box, waiting to rehearse the second act, she got her first glimpse of the Maestro in action. The stage was set as the dining room of a stately old Virginian mansion.

Suddenly, Belasco interrupted the actors with a roar that jolted Mary upright. "Hold everything!" he yelled. He stormed onto the stage, demanding to know what was in one of the props, a jar, that in the script was supposed to contain molasses. "Taste it," he ordered the stage manager. "Tell me what that is."

When the trembling manager admitted that it was actually maple syrup, Belasco seized the jar and threw it to the floor, smashing it to pieces. Then he proceeded to jump up and down in the sticky mess, grinding it into the Oriental carpet.

That accomplished, he strode over to the box where Mary sat wide-eyed, holding her breath. To her surprise, he asked her what she thought of his performance.

"I think I may have missed my calling, Betty," he said, with a twinkle in his eye. He would always refer to her by the name of her character in his play. "I should have been an actor, don't you agree?" Mary was at a loss for words.

Appreciating what an opportunity it was to work for David Belasco, Mary never stopped trying to improve her performance, reading and re-reading her lines until she'd decided on the best way to deliver them. She watched the more experienced actors closely and learned whatever she could from them.

Mary later credited the time spent with Belasco for teaching her how to act with heart and feeling, and his advice to "always keep it natural" seemed to echo Charlotte's earlier words.

On his part, Belasco was impressed by the way the fifteen-year-old was able to visualize the story and illustrate it with her facial expressions, or with very subtle body movements. Mary was graceful and appeared relaxed, and Belasco seemed to recognize a star quality in her.

Early on, Mary told Belasco that she'd feel more comfortable in her role as Betty Warren if she had a doll to play with on the stage. She was touched that the man went out and bought her a doll with a china head, like the one she'd told him she remembered from childhood. The doll became a treasured memento that Mary kept for the rest of her life.

On December 3, 1907, *The Warrens of Virginia* opened on Broadway at the Belasco Theatre. It was a magnificent theatre — a far cry from the rickety, dirty theatres of Gladys Smith's barnstorming days.

She loved the sight of the well-dressed audience on the other side of the footlights: the women in their evening gowns, and the men, elegant in their white shirts and waistcoats. She breathed in the perfume that wafted up to her on the stage.

Mary saved the price of streetcar fare by walking to and from the theatre every day. Her pay, at $25 a week, was less than she had earned working in stock, but she felt the prestige of appearing in a Belasco production made any sacrifice worthwhile.

The production ran on Broadway until May 16, 1908. It played for a second season on the road, opening in Boston September 21, 1908, and closing March 20, 1909, with a five-day engagement at the West End Theatre in Harlem.

During its touring season, the company had only one week off at Christmas, and then they were back on the road again. They played Toronto at the Royal Alexandra Theatre in January 1909, before returning to the U.S. The Toronto critics made a fuss about Mary's homecoming, remarking on how, after ten years behind the footlights, she spoke and carried herself like an adult.

Warrens played a total of 190 performances. For as long as it was on the road, Mary was paid an extra $5 a week on top of her regular earnings. Her touring roommate was a novice actress named Blanche Yurka. Mary was able to pass on to Blanche some of the tips she'd learned about how to get the most for her money and how to save by doubling up on hotel rooms. The two girls ate bananas with milk for breakfast because the restaurants only charged five cents for it. For the entire run of the play, Mary lived on $5 a week and sent the rest back to Charlotte.

Unfortunately, David Belasco had no work for Mary when the season was over. She promised him that if he ever wanted her again, no matter where she was or what she was doing, he had only to ask, and she would come.

When *The Warrens of Virginia* ended its run, the Pickford family, as they now called themselves, was reunited in New York. Charlotte was just managing to survive, playing in the city in a Chauncey Olcott production, *Ragged Robin*, in which Jack and Lottie, too, had bit parts.

But, for a while, the family had enough money to buy food and pay the overdue rent on their West 17th Street boarding house. They even allowed themselves to purchase some new clothes. Still, the summer, the down season, was ahead. Unless they went back to barnstorming, there might not be any work until September. Going back on the road would undoubtedly mean that they would be separated into different stock companies.

It was while she'd been in Chicago, touring with one of the early stock productions, that Mary had first seen moving pictures, or "flickers," as they were known in the early days.

Hale's Tours and Scenes of the World, first exhibited at the St. Louis Expo in 1904, had been showing in all the large American cities by this time. These travel films were shown in tiny theatres built to resemble railway coaches. Inside the coach, the "conductor" took the tickets from the platform, and the audience sat on old streetcar or train seats. The lights went out, and the whole coach swayed as if it were taking its passengers on a real journey, while the film was projected onto a small screen at the front.

To film the motion picture, the camera had been mounted on the platform of a moving train as it sped through tunnels and raced around sharp curves. The audience in the theatre had the sensation of being on that speeding train.

That, coupled with the dark, and the smells of other people in the stifling, cramped space, caused Mary to be overcome with motion sickness. By the time she stumbled back outside, she wanted nothing more to do with moving pictures.

But Jack and Lottie, according to their older sister, became almost addicted to the flickers. Every time they had five or ten cents, they'd rush off to a store on West 23rd Street in New York City to see a film.

Other than *Hale's Tours* and their railway coaches, the flickers were most often shown in converted storefronts, their plate glass windows covered over on the inside with posters. These makeshift theatres were called "nickelodeons," because the price of admission was usually a nickel. For five cents, you might see three reels of film and an illustrated song.

Often located in poor, downtown neighbourhoods, nickelodeons were potential fire traps, as the seating was a collection of old chairs or anything else that could be assembled for the purpose. The films were projected on a sheet hung at the front for a screen, and someone would bang away on a piano to provide musical accompaniment to match the action in the film.

Mary believed that nice people didn't go to nickelodeons. Theatre actors, like herself, considered the flickers "low class." And to *play* in a moving picture would only be the final choice for a desperate actor who'd run out of options.

But demand for films had become huge. In 1909 there were thousands of nickelodeons in America, each one showing a variety of subjects on short films. The programs, which usually ran for an hour or an hour and a half, changed daily.

Charlotte had been listening to some of the cast members in Olcott's production talk about how they'd worked the previous summer at Biograph, the leading film company in New York. Apparently, it was possible to make a quick $5 a day there.

Whereas the stock companies shut down for the summer because the theatres they played in got too hot, the voracious appetite created by the nickelodeons meant filming went on year round.

Charlotte broached the subject to her eldest daughter. "Would you be very much against applying for work at the Biograph studio, Gladdie?"

Go into the movies? Mary was incredulous. How demeaning! She was a Belasco actress; movies were beneath her dignity.

But a job in moving pictures would mean the four of them could stay together in New York for the summer, and Charlotte wasn't long in pointing that out. Besides, she said, "They pay as much as five dollars a day, Gladdie."

Charlotte wasn't above a little bribery. If Mary would agree to try her luck at Biograph, her mother would allow her to wear a pair of silk stockings for the first time. And a pair of high-heeled shoes.

Because she always obeyed Charlotte, Mary swallowed her pride. She dressed in her navy blue serge suit, striped shirtwaist, a new, rolled-brim straw hat, and boarded the streetcar to West 14th Street.

In order to spend only one nickel on the cross-town trolley, she had planned her route to the Biograph studio very carefully. Why would she waste precious money on such a pointless trip, anyway? She would step inside the hated studio, pay the call as she'd promised her mother she would, and get out of there as quickly as possible.

4

The Flickers

The American Mutoscope and Biograph Company (more often known simply as Biograph) was housed in a four-storey brownstone building on East 14th Street in New York City. Inside the double front doors of this former mansion was a large, marble-floored foyer and a set of steps that led to the main floor. The studio itself, once an elegant ballroom, was at the end of a long hall, lined on either side by offices.

The chief director at Biograph, David Wark Griffith, had been with the company for about a year when Mary arrived. He was thirty-three. Griffith had worked as an actor, but what he really wanted was to be was a playwright. He'd sold the occasional story synopsis to Biograph, done a bit of acting for them, and almost by accident, become a director, having taken over for another of the company's directors who had fallen ill. Now, apparently, he had found his niche.

The permanent acting company at Biograph included Mack Sennett; Florence Lawrence, a Hamilton, Ontario, native known as the "Biograph Girl"; Lawrence's husband, Harry Solter; Kate Bruce; and a handsome young Irishman by the name of Owen Moore.

Arriving at the studio that April morning in 1909, Mary hoped that the people in the casting office wouldn't want her, and that none of her theatre friends would see her entering the building.

Interestingly, Mary had already thought of finding work in the flickers, but she'd kept that search a secret. In 1907 she'd dropped into the offices of the Kalem studio in New York, looking for work. Finding no one around, she'd quickly left. In Chicago Mary and another young actress had ventured into the Essanay studio, but they'd gotten no farther than the dark and scary-looking entrance to the building, where they'd both lost their nerve.

Mary was not surprised when the person behind the desk in the Biograph casting office told her they had no work for her. She was on her way out again when a tall, thin man with a hawk-like nose stepped in front of her. He introduced himself as D.W. Griffith.

"Are you an actress?" he demanded, in a sonorous tone.

"I most certainly am, sir."

"What experience, *if any*, have you had, if I may ask?"

Mary drew herself up to her full five feet and one quarter inch. "*Only* ten years in the theatre, sir. And two of them with David Belasco."

"Well, you're too little and too fat," Griffith declared. "But I may decide to give you a chance, regardless. I'm looking for someone of your type for my next picture." Griffith had recently begun to introduce young women with Mary's delicate grace into his films.

"If the salary is right," Mary said.

Griffith offered to take her on trial and guaranteed three days' work each week at $5 a day.

Mary coolly informed the man that she must have $10 a day.

"Five dollars for today, then," Griffith countered, "and ten for tomorrow."

"I am a Belasco actress, sir," Mary reiterated. "I must have a guarantee of $25 per week, and extra when I work extra."

Intrigued by the nerve of the girl, Griffith said he'd have to check with the front office. The amount could possibly be arranged, but she mustn't tell the other actors.

There must have been some mutual respect between them, because D.W. Griffith agreed to give Mary a screen test. He took her to the women's dressing room first. It was a large room, divided down the middle by one long, shelf-like dressing table. Later, Mary would learn that one side of the dressing table was designated for newcomers and less well-known actresses; the other side was for the important actresses and the veterans. Also on this side of the room were two individual dressing tables, reserved for the stars of the company.

Griffith himself applied Mary's makeup for her screen test — the heavy whiteface and black eyeliner, the exaggerated black eyebrows. In silent films the story had to be conveyed in pantomime, and expressive use of the eyebrows was crucial. Even the actors' hands would be dusted with white chalk, so that the camera would not miss a gesture.

After hunting down a makeshift costume from the wardrobe department in the cellar, Griffith led Mary into the studio. Without bothering to introduce her to the other actors gathered there, he told her what he wanted her to do. She was screen testing for a part in the film *Pippa Passes*.

Someone handed Mary a mandolin, and Griffith told her to walk across the set, improvise some dialogue, and act as if she were strumming the instrument and singing.

The camera began to roll. Mary was concentrating on all the instructions, when suddenly one of the other actors, Owen Moore, asked, "Who's the dame?"

Mary stopped dead in her tracks. He was referring to her! She forgot the camera, the mandolin, and her grotesque makeup. And she forgot director D.W. Griffith.

Mary, whose idea of a dame was a woman of loose moral standards, was highly indignant, and she lashed out angrily at the other actor: "How dare you call me a bad name! I'm a perfectly respectable girl. How dare you insult me, sir!"

Griffith let out a ferocious roar. "You've ruined it!" he bellowed. "Do you know how much film cost per foot, Miss … Miss whatever-your-name-is? Never, as long as you live, do a thing like that again. Now, start again from the beginning."

When Owen Moore protested that he'd meant no harm by his remark, Mary realized that "dame" must have a different meaning from the one she was aware of.

She crossed the stage and began again. It was past eight o'clock that evening by the time she was finally able to take off the hideous makeup and prepare to leave. She knew she'd likely failed her screen test, and that she had ruined any chance of being in the flickers. She might as well go home and forget about it.

She was surprised to find D.W. Griffith waiting for her outside. So much for a hasty exit. "Would you care to have dinner with me tonight?" the director asked.

Stunned, Mary declined. She'd never in her entire life had dinner with a man, let alone one of Mr. Griffith's age. As she was leaving the building, it began to rain, and Mr. Griffith insisted on walking her, under the shelter of his umbrella, to the subway. There he left her and said, "Till tomorrow, at nine sharp."

Mary was soaked through by the time she arrived at the theatre in Brooklyn where Charlotte was finishing the run of the Olcott play. She found Jack asleep in the dressing room, curled up on top of the family's trunk. Charlotte and Lottie were still on stage.

Mary's brand new shoes were ruined, as was her $3.50 hat. She was still clutching the sodden $5 bill she'd earned for the day. Shivering, Mary sat and waited for the rest of the family.

When Charlotte came in with Lottie, she hung up Mary's wet clothes and spread the $5 bill on the radiator to dry. Mary's teeth were still chattering. "They're going to pay me $10 a day from now on," she said.

The next morning, filled with dread, Mary walked the whole way to the studio, refusing to part with the streetcar fare. She would do this thing, but only because it was an economic necessity, a means of keeping her family together.

Mary Pickford made her film debut on April 20, 1909, just after her seventeenth birthday. She had a tiny role, that of a ten-year-old child in *Her First Biscuits*. Featuring Florence Lawrence, the film was a seven-minute split-reel comedy.

Comedies and slapstick were usually in this split-reel format, using reels that contained two short films, each running 500 feet. Dramas were most often 1,000 feet of film — a full reel.

The studio in the converted ballroom at Biograph, so dark and noisy, was unfamiliar territory to Mary. Every bit of sunlight had to be shut out during the filming. Two dozen arc lights, hung on pulleys, surrounded the studio, and there were banks of Cooper-Hewitts, the mercury-vapour lamps that turned the actors' faces green and gave them purple lips. On film, however, they would appear perfectly normal. The noise of the camera, shooting out sprockets as it filmed, was deafening.

The films of D.W. Griffith were recognized as the best in the business at that time, better than those from any other production house in America. One could count on Griffith's films to be funnier or more melodramatic than the run-of-the-mill pictures. Mary was impressed with the way Griffith and Billy Bitzer, his cameraman, could come up with so many different sets in the old ballroom.

Still, the studio would get so hot from the mercury-vapour lamps and the flaming arcs that it was a treat for the company to go off to film at one of Griffith's favourite outdoor locations. Places like Fort Lee in New Jersey or Cuddebackville in New York provided him with the fields and brooks and wooded hillsides he preferred to use as background.

It didn't take Mary long to discover just how busy she was going to be at Biograph. The dailies, also called the rushes, which were the unedited print of all the shots taken for a film, were shown in one of the upstairs bedrooms of the house, and everyone was encouraged to give his free and honest opinion of what had been filmed that day.

At first it had been a shock to Mary how the camera made her appear heavier than she was. At 115 pounds, Mary was the picture of youthful good health. She would later try to maintain a weight closer to ninety-five pounds on her tiny frame.

Mondays at the Biograph studio were usually spent in rehearsal. Griffith would have everyone gather around the camera platform, where he would explain the premise of the story they were going to film and ask for suggestions on how to flesh it out. When that had been decided upon, he would go around the circle of players. "How do you like that, Pickford? All right with you, Moore?" And the parts would be assigned.

Gradually, Mary began to feel that she was part of the company. One of the first things that struck her as unusual at Biograph was how all the actors called one another by their first names. She wasn't used to such familiarity, having always been addressed by the other Belasco actors as Miss Pickford. At Biograph Mr. Griffith was the exception; he was always Mr. Griffith (or D.W., behind his back), but he called the members of his company by their last names only.

Just as they had in the theatre, the Biograph actors applied their own makeup. Costumes were made from whatever was available on the costume rack or often came from the actors' own wardrobes. Mary was so much smaller than the other women in the company that she would have to be pinned into costumes originally made to fit larger actresses. In order to hide the pins, she had to make sure she never turned her back to the camera.

D.W. Griffith was fascinated by the challenge of the new medium of motion pictures, and because he gave his actors, including Mary, a personal interest in the films that they made together, they shared his vision of what movies could become.

No one was typecast at Biograph. An actor could play the lead one day and have a bit part the next. Early on, Mary played a child in a couple of films, but her usual roles were those of girls of her own age, sixteen- to twenty-year-olds.

By giving his actors a variety of roles — the lead one day, a walk-on the next — Griffith kept the cost of labour down. If no one was sure of being a star, no one would be demanding star wages. But from the beginning, Mary dreamed of getting one of the two individual tables on the more prestigious side of the dressing room as her own.

Although she respected Mr. Griffith as an artist, Mary would not give in to him on every issue. They were both dominant personalities, and they had frequent, heated arguments, sometimes resulting in the director firing the girl, only to rehire her an hour later.

On Tuesdays at Biograph, they shot the interior scenes; on Wednesdays, the exteriors. They worked from 9 a.m. to 8 p.m. and were paid at the end of each day. There was a forty-five-minute break for lunch, and that was usually eaten on the set.

If they had a spell of rainy weather during filming, the company would complete the interiors for several pictures while they waited for the sun to reappear. As soon as it did, D.W. Griffith and his actors would hurry out and shoot the exteriors. They had to adhere to a tight schedule, committed as they were to getting two or three pictures out every week.

In 1909, in order to have something to film, someone had to make up a story or adapt it from another work. Since the films were distributed to five-cent nickelodeons, where the story came from didn't seem to matter much — even if it had been stolen.

These screen stories, or scenarios as they were called, often came from the actors themselves. Even Mary tried her hand at writing scenarios, and she managed to sell "Lena and the Geese" and "Madame Rex" to Mr. Griffith for $15 each.

Making a silent film involved no specific dialogue; the actors usually improvised. In fact, if the camera happened to film something interesting off stage, that, too, might find its way into the picture. The cameraman was all-important. Besides shooting the film, it was his job to take care of the lighting and the scenery.

By the time Mary made her 1909 debut, D.W. Griffith had made over 110 short films, and he and Billy Bitzer were continually experimenting with new camera and lighting techniques.

Although Mary was still a young girl, the director had decided it was time for her to portray more mature roles. "Would you like to play the lead tomorrow, Pickford?" Griffith asked one day.

"Yes, sir," Mary replied.

In that case, he asked, had she ever played a love scene? Did she even know how?

Mary, who had never been on a date, let alone kissed a boy, assured him that of course she knew how.

"Prove it for me, then," Griffith challenged, and he immediately hailed a prop boy who happened to be passing by, carrying a papier-mâché pillar. "Hold on a second with that, will you?" he said.

"Now Mary," he said. "I want you to pretend that pillar is the leading man. I want you to show me how you'd make love to him."

"Please, Mr. Griffith," Mary begged, embarrassed beyond description, and hoping to escape such humiliation. "Do you really expect me to play a love scene with a stone-cold pillar?"

Just as that moment, a handsome young actor emerged from the mens' dressing room. It was Owen Moore, the man who had earlier called her a "dame," and a man who was destined to be part of a sad chapter in Mary's life.

Griffith called Owen over. "Listen, Moore. Pickford here doesn't want to make love to a lifeless pillar. Let's see if she can do better with you."

Mary was so mortified she wanted to walk out. If it weren't for the money she was going to be paid, she would have.

She thought back to how she'd seen people in the theatre "make love" and decided the way to do it was to look lovingly into the man's eyes. There would be no kissing; she had been taught by Charlotte that kissing in public was vulgar. Besides, in the theatre it wasn't necessary; one could just pretend.

Mary managed to get through the scene, although her heart was hammering so hard when Owen Moore put his arms around her that she thought he must be able to hear it. She pressed her face against his chest, and Moore was gallant enough to play along with the frightened young girl.

Mr. Griffith was satisfied. Mary got the lead opposite Moore in *The Violin Maker of Cremona*. It was a one-reel melodrama, and D.W. Griffith was so pleased with Mary that he offered her a contract of up to $40 a week.

Although they were often at odds with each other, Griffith was particularly protective of Mary. She was his youngest actress, and he assumed an almost father-like role with her. Whenever the company stayed overnight on location, he made sure that Mary had a room across from his own.

As an example of the preferential treatment Mary would occasionally receive, Griffith once gave his wife, actress Linda Arvidson, $20 from the Biograph petty cash to buy the girl something to wear for her part in *The Lonely Villa*, a film that was to be shot on location in Fort Lee, New Jersey. Mary was to play a girl of thirteen, a member of a wealthy family, and she had no clothes of her own that were suitable for the role.

The state of New Jersey offered a wide variety of scenery for location shoots, including farms, woods, and rural countryside along the Passaic River. Little Falls, where *They Would Elope* was filmed, provided large, elegant homes as background for the picture and local people who could be hired as extras. The

Biograph Company also filmed at locations in Connecticut and New York.

If they were shooting on location, each actor was responsible for packing his own costume and makeup into a prop wagon, and the wagon, carrying the cameras as well as the props, would leave New York the night before the shoot.

The actors would get up early in the morning and take the subway to the ferry. A couple of hotel rooms would have been rented for the group, where they could get into their costumes and apply their makeup. Horse-drawn buggies would then transport the actors to the location, all ready for filming.

In 1909 Mary Pickford played forty-five roles for Griffith and another thirty-five in 1910. With her sweet smile, her perkiness, and her long, golden ringlets, Mary was winning hearts at the nickelodeons and being noticed by the critics. By the time she'd made her twelfth picture with Biograph, she had enough clout with the company to get small parts for Lottie and Jack.

These early films, often single reels of fifteen to twenty minutes in length, took only a day or two to shoot. Filming was fast, and re-takes too expensive and time-consuming to consider.

The movies told simple stories filmed in wide shots so that the actors were seen from head-to-toe. Inter-titles, just enough words to explain what could not be shown by means of mime, were written after the film was edited. ("Meanwhile, in a nearby town, three scoundrels were plotting.")

Silent films were never meant to be seen in silence. They were accompanied by live music played on the organ, or the piano, or sometimes by a full pit orchestra. As well as setting the mood for the scenes, the music helped to mask the sound of the noisy projectors in the back of the theatre.

D.W. Griffith seemed to like casting Mary Pickford as Indian or Mexican women. To get the right look, Mary would have to apply thick red clay to her arms and legs with a sponge. She would then don a black wig made of horsehair and a heavy beaded dress that weighed down her small frame.

Coming from the theatre, Mary's style of acting was restrained, but Mr. Griffith wanted her to be more melodramatic. Once, he grabbed her by the shoulders, hard, and shook her.

"Get some feeling into you, Pickford!" he shouted into her face.

Mary promptly bent her head and bit him. She was as surprised at her reaction as Griffith was, and more so when her sister, Lottie, who was also in the studio, flew onto the set, jumped onto the man's back, and started pulling his ears. "How dare you do that to my sister!" Lottie screamed. Griffith shook himself free.

"What gave you the right to lay your hands on me, sir?" Mary said. "If I am not an actress, you cannot shake it into me. I'm finished with you and with motion pictures." She fled the stage and ran out of the building.

True to form, D.W. Griffith caught up with her outside and apologized for his behaviour. He begged her to come back, and grudgingly Mary returned to finish the scene.

"Come on, now," Griffith shouted. "Let me see the real Pickford!" The camera began to roll.

Mary was so distraught by what had just occurred between them that tears began streaming down her face. And Mr. Griffith got the shot he'd been looking for.

Part of the problem, which this episode illustrates, was that Griffith expected his actors to use the elaborate gestures from the French school of pantomime. Mary refused to exaggerate, remembering her mother's advice to "feel" the part and Belasco's that she should keep it natural. She informed Griffith that actors in the movies, being so much closer to the audience than was possible on the stage, should scale down their performances.

Mary chose to show emotion in her films by using subtle, natural gestures. She had mastered the art of facial expression, and Griffith had finally to admit that she *did* seem to have a special relationship with the camera. Coming into the business when she did, Mary Pickford invented the art of acting in motion pictures.

Critics praised Griffith's new ingenue, especially her charm and simple style. After only three months, movie goers were starting to recognize the "Girl with the Curls," as they referred to her, or "Goldilocks."

The *New York Dramatic Mirror,* in a review on August 21, 1909, of *They Would Elope,* singled Mary out: "This delicious little comedy introduces again an ingénue whose work in Biograph pictures is attracting attention."

But who was she? What was her name? Only the director's name appeared on the film credits; the actors themselves, in those days, were anonymous.

In England, where moviegoers also wondered who this delightful young actress was, they gave her a name of their own. They called her "Dorothy Nicholson."

Aware of Mary's growing following, Griffith put Jack and Lottie on the official payroll and promised to cast Mary in leading roles, hoping to keep her happy. He also raised her salary to $100 dollars a week — unheard of for a seventeen-year-old actress. Now the Pickford family was able to rent a comfortable apartment and to save toward a holiday.

D.W. Griffith bought three of Mary's screen stories in 1909, and Mack Sennett, another Canadian-born member of the company who was writing scenarios, suggested to her that Mary was having her stories accepted on the strength of her long, blond hair.

Sennett, born in the Eastern Townships of Quebec, had moved to the U.S. when he was seventeen. He would later be a co-founder of Keystone Studios in Endale, California, and would be credited with inventing slapstick.

Sennett asked Mary if he could put her name to one of his scenarios to try to prove his point. If it sold, he told her he'd pay her a commission of $5 for a split reel, or $8 for a full reel.

Mary agreed on the condition that she read Sennett's story before signing her name to it. When he brought her the first one, and it involved a group of totally inept policemen acting in an outrageous fashion, she refused to endorse it.

"If you expect me to put my name to that story," she said, "you'll have to change all those policemen into private detectives. Their behaviour is scandalous!"

Sennett wouldn't make the change. He put his own name on it, and the scenario became the first of the very successful Keystone Cops films. It was not one of Mary's most astute business decisions.

When Florence Lawrence and her husband left Biograph to work for Carl Laemmle's Independent Motion Picture Company (IMP), Griffith gave Lawrence's coveted individual dressing table to Mary. In her mind at least, she was now a star.

Late one afternoon, while Griffith was directing a picture called *Friends*, starring Mary and Lionel Barrymore, he decided to experiment. He asked Billy Bitzer to move the camera. The camera, which usually filmed from a fixed position, stood about five feet high and weighed 300 pounds. According to Mary, Bitzer used to keep his lunch inside it.

"Come on, Billy," Griffith urged, "let's have some fun! Move the camera up and get closer to Mary."

Later Mary wrote that this was the first screen close-up (actually a semi close-up that cut her at the waist) and was very different from the norm in cinematography.

When the front office chiefs at Biograph saw the results, they were not enthusiastic. "We're paying this girl the large sum of $100 per week," they said. "We want to be able to see all of her. Including her feet."

Although Griffith understood that the bosses wanted their money's worth, he ignored them, and he went on to master other new techniques in cinematography. These included fade-outs, where the closing scene in a movie fades to black, and fade-ins, the mechanical reverse. He also introduced the tracking shot, in which the camera moves along with the action; for example, the camera might follow the path of a plate that someone has thrown as it leaves the person's hand, moves through the air, and smashes against the wall. This innovative technique would eventually become a staple of the industry.

Whenever Mary's part in a picture was finished for the day, she would stay and watch the others in their scenes. She was never intrusive. Instead, she watched quietly from the sidelines. Some might say she was aloof, but she was taking it all in. Mary, determined to learn all she could about the business, never stopped listening and observing. She had entered the film making industry in its infancy and was ready to learn all the new techniques as they developed. She studied editing, lighting, and how the camera worked, and because she was so quick to learn, she became Billy Bitzer's favourite actress.

As Mary later phrased it, "It was very exciting. There we were, pioneers in a brand new medium of art."

5

A Wedding in Secret

Owen Moore was born in Ireland in 1886 and raised in Toledo, Ohio. One of four brothers, all of whom worked in the movies, he started to work for Biograph just five months before Mary Pickford arrived. He was a handsome man, tall, with a rosy complexion, dark hair, deep blue eyes, and perfect teeth. Mary used to refer to him as the "Beau Brummell of Biograph," because he was always so elegantly dressed.

The man also had a dark side — a quick temper and a serious drinking problem that affected his work. On occasion, he would disappear altogether from the set without telling anyone where he was going, and no one would be able to find him.

Mary had been infatuated with Owen Moore from the first time he'd put his arms around her, for the infamous love scene. She tried to keep her feelings to herself. She didn't think the man, who was several years older than she was, even noticed her that first summer at Biograph.

She considered actor James Kirkwood as her first real friend in the company. Not as handsome as Owen Moore, the man was, nonetheless, tall and distinguished-looking, and he and Mary remained friends all their lives. Kirkwood was playing leads for D.W. Griffith shortly after starting in films in 1909. By 1912 he'd turned to directing and would go on to direct nine of Mary Pickford's movies, co-starring with her in three.

Mary's crush on Owen Moore, not as well-hidden as she'd hoped, became a cause for concern among the others in the company. It was the studio carpenter who took it upon himself to speak to her one day, warning her about Moore, suggesting that the man wasn't right for her.

"I hate to tell you this, Mary," the carpenter said. "But I've seen him in wardrobe, sleeping off the effects of 'a beer too many' at Luchow's."

Mary had guessed that Owen might be a drinker, but she was so much in love with him that she was willing to overlook it. Besides, he was only one of many actors in the Biograph Company who drank. Alcoholism seemed to be an occupational hazard.

Before long, Owen Moore started coming around to the Pickford apartment to see Mary. At first Charlotte thought it was harmless. Because Mary was so young, she thought Moore would soon lose interest in the girl. It might have continued in this way for some time if someone at Biograph had not warned Charlotte that things between Mary and Owen Moore were getting too serious and that Moore had a reputation as a ladies' man.

Immediately, Charlotte informed Mary that Owen was no longer welcome in their home, and she forbade her daughter to see him anywhere, other than at work. As should have been expected, Charlotte's position only made matters worse, and for the first time in her life, Mary disobeyed her mother. She and Owen Moore began to meet in secret.

In January 1910, D.W. Griffith surprised everyone with the announcement that he had persuaded his superiors at Biograph to let him take a select group to California in order to escape the brutal New York winter. The group included Frank Powell (as co-manager and assistant director), Griffith himself, two cameramen, a prop boy, and a number of Biograph's chief actors, including seventeen-year-old Mary Pickford, Mack Sennett, Henry Waltham, and Billy Quirk. The previous autumn, Mary had made a series of comedies known as "the Muggsy films" with Quirk.

Owen Moore had hoped to be included in the group, but he had made the mistake of first asking that he be given a raise in pay. Griffith refused and took Moore's name off the list of those heading to California.

Young Jack Pickford wanted to go along too, and he complained to Mr. Griffith about not being chosen. Griffith had no intention of sending the boy, and Mary didn't want the nuisance of having her kid brother tagging along. But at the last minute, just as the train carrying the company was pulling out of the station, Charlotte shoved Jack on board, instructing the fourteen-year-old to look after his sister.

Finding himself finally free of his mother's control, Jack went a little wild in sunny California. More than once, Mary had to pay to get him out of trouble, and she wished she'd left him at home.

The move out west might have been just the thing to cool the ardour between Mary and Owen, and it has been suggested that Charlotte had made a deal with Mr. Griffith to keep Moore back in New York.

Although Broadway was the centre for the American entertainment industry in 1910, the Los Angeles Chamber of Commerce was trying to entice the motion picture companies to come to the sunny south, where filming on location was possible all year round. One film company, Spoor and Anderson, better known as Essanay, had already set up shop there.

In 1910 the village of Los Angeles was linked to the tiny suburb of Hollywood by a dirt road with the grandiose name of Sunset Boulevard. The streets of Hollywood were unpaved, and the gardens spilled right onto the roadway. It was a place of sagebrush and swaying palms, of fields filled with tall grass and an abundance of wildflowers, and Beverly Hills was inhabited only by the deer and coyotes. But with the Chamber's promise of 350 days of sunshine per year, the area was bound to attract other movie companies before long.

The Biograph studio in Los Angeles was a one-acre vacant lot on the corner of Grand and Washington streets. It was wide open, without roof or walls, although there was a fence separating it from the adjacent lumberyard and a small baseball diamond. Many curious kids would scale the fence in order to watch what was going on at the movie lot next door.

The studio set was a large wooden platform with a revolving shed that could be turned to take full advantage of the sun. On windy days, the curtains that were strung up to provide the shed with walls would billow and flap.

Without the luxury of dressing rooms, the actors put their costumes on before leaving their hotel each morning. Looking back years later, Mary remarked that in the early days with Biograph, the actors wore the same costume throughout the entire picture.

Rehearsals were held in the loft of an old rented building on Main Street. This was where the company also stored its props and developed its films. In the evening, the company would gather in the loft to watch the dailies and prepare for the next day's filming.

As always, Mr. Griffith welcomed everyone's story ideas, and Mary came up with *May and December*, for which he paid her $15. When he rejected her next two scenarios, a 1,000-foot story and a split-reel comedy, Mary and her brother, Jack, rented a pair of horses and rode out to see Mr. Spoor of Essanay. He bought both of Mary's screen stories, making her $40 richer.

Mary had made a stringent budget for Jack and herself to live on while they were in California, and the extra income from the sale of her stories was most welcome. Fortunately, it wasn't long before Jack, too, was able to contribute to the family purse. Griffith decided to make use of the boy while he was there, and Jack was paid the standard $5 a day as a stunt man. He fell off horses and got thrown through windows for all the young actresses in the company.

By spring the two Pickfords had saved a total of $1,200, which they looked forward to turning over to Charlotte when they got home.

During the stay in California, Griffith took part of the company to the San Gabriel Mission to film *The Thread of Destiny*, a melodrama in which Mary played the part of an orphan. Also in California, she made *Ramona*, one of her most famous films. Biograph put out a special brochure to advertise the lavish production, which was set against the magnificent palisades of Ventura County, California.

Mary had had three months on the West Coast, away from Owen Moore — plenty of time to think about her relationship with him. Now, with the stay nearly over, she could hardly wait to get home to see him again.

The company arrived back in New York in April 1910. Throughout the summer and fall of that year, Mary and Owen spent what time they could together. They could not have kept their love affair secret from Charlotte had they not enlisted the help of some of the other actors in the company.

But all the deception was taking its toll on Mary. She was depressed and anxious. When she told Owen, in tears, that she felt miserable sneaking around and lying to her mother, he asked her to marry him. Mary turned him down.

She was, by that time, Biograph's leading lady. She had inherited the title "The Biograph Girl," and she was well-liked by the other actors. But she was growing a little restless, thinking it might be time to move on.

Biograph had always stuck to the practice, used by most of the studios, of keeping the names of its actors from the public. But when Florence Lawrence went to IMP, that company bucked tradition and put Lawrence's name on the film credits.

Meanwhile, Charlotte was busy behind the scenes, making contract negotiations with Carl Laemmle of IMP on Mary's behalf. Florence Lawrence left that company in 1910 for the Lubin studio, and now IMP was ready to attract a new star.

IMP's offer to Mary was for $175 a week, and she would have featured billing as "Little Mary." Owen Moore had already signed with IMP, having left Biograph after Griffith refused to give him a raise and take him to California. He, too, was urging Mary to join the company, and for once, Charlotte agreed with the man.

Mary was well aware that Biograph was making the best pictures in America, but regardless, she signed with IMP in

December 1910. The other three Pickfords were also hired, as atmospheric (background) actors.

Mary began her stay with the new company in a picture called *Their First Misunderstanding*. It was directed by Thomas Ince, and Owen was her leading man.

All the while, Owen was keeping up his pressure on eighteen-year-old Mary to marry him, threatening to go away and never see her again if she refused.

She felt helpless in the face of this ultimatum. On January 7, 1911, Mary borrowed a long dress with a train from the wardrobe mistress at the studio, telling her she needed it for a party and, wrapped in her mother's over-sized coat, she and Owen took the ferry over to the courthouse in Jersey City.

"If ever there was a sadder wedding I have yet to hear of it," Mary later wrote.

Even as she walked through the drizzle, in the cold January night, she was struck by the fact that she really didn't want to be there. She didn't want to leave her family. Why, she hardly knew Owen Moore. Could she possibly run fast enough to make it to the subway station before he could, she wondered. But she was wearing wobbly, high-heeled shoes and had no money for subway fare.

Within a few minutes, she and Owen Moore were married. After the wedding, he took her back to her family's apartment. They said good night at the door, and Owen left. Mary went inside and crawled into the double bed she shared with her sister, Lottie.

For weeks the newlyweds told no one they were married. For everyone except Mary, who felt "guilty of a monstrous betrayal" to her family, life went on as if nothing had happened.

* * *

An ugly situation was brewing between the companies who were part of the Motion Picture Patents Company (MPPC), known as "the Trust," and were thereby licensed to use Thomas Edison's patented movie camera, and those independents who were not. Biograph was part of MPPC, but IMP was not.

In an effort to avoid any trouble — already some thugs had been hired to smash the cameras and rough up the actors at IMP — the company decided to ship its whole crew to Cuba for three months. Before they sailed, Owen insisted that Mary use the time at sea to tell her family about their marriage. Then, perhaps, they could turn the Cuban junket into a honeymoon. It turned out to be a nightmare.

When Mary finally broke the news, Charlotte cried for three days straight, and neither Jack nor Lottie would speak to their sister. The sight of Jack, standing at the rail of the ship, holding his little dog in his arms and sobbing, broke Mary's heart. For years afterward, she would torture herself with the memory of that scene. She felt like the greatest sinner who'd ever lived; she had let her whole family down.

The heat and humidity in Cuba were oppressive, and the actors grew listless. What little food they got to eat was terrible. One day Thomas Ince's assistant, a man by the name of North, said something rude to Mary, and Owen promptly attacked him. Someone called the police, but before they could get there, Charlotte took control of the situation.

She persuaded some of the other actors to hide Owen from the authorities until he could be safely shipped out of the country. The next morning, Mary joined her husband on a boat in Havana Harbour, and they returned together to the United States.

It hadn't taken long for Mary to discover that Owen was not only jealous of other men where she was concerned, he was also jealous of her family. Compounding the problem was his resentment over the fact that his wife was earning more money than he was.

On the surface, when he was sober, Owen Moore was a quiet man, although sometimes given to moody silences. It was when he'd been drinking that his temper would flare. The couple's quarrels increased in frequency, although, according to Mary, they never quarrelled in public.

Mary knew that IMP's films were not very good, and she longed to go back to Biograph. Nine months into her contract with IMP, she became sick — whether physically ill or just sick of working with IMP is open to question — and used this as grounds for cancelling her contract. She had made thirty-three pictures with Carl Laemmle's company in that time.

When IMP later took Mary to court for breach of contract, it was only the fact that she'd been underage when she signed with them that got her off without a stiff penalty.

Next, she signed with Harry Aitkens of Majestic Pictures, a company that was formed for her. Majestic agreed to Mary's request that Owen be given the chance to direct, and he and Mary made *The Courtship of Mary* together in 1911. Owen Moore was never to know that his employment was a condition of Mary's contract with Majestic. During her short stay with the company, she made five pictures, with a salary of $225 per week.

In 1912 Mary went back to Biograph, and Owen signed with Victor Films. Mary took a cut in pay, but she was glad to be back, so much so that she burst into tears of relief when she saw Mr. Griffith again.

In the summer of 1912, the Gish sisters, Lillian and Dorothy, who were still touring in the theatre, recognized their friend in the comedy *Lena and the Geese*, which was showing in Baltimore while they were there. Mary was not only the star of the picture but also its author.

The sisters went home and told their mother that they'd just seen Gladys Smith in the flickers. What a comedown for the Smith family!

When the Gishes got to New York, they went to Biograph, looking for their old friend. They were surprised to discover that Gladys Smith was no more and that Mary Pickford had taken her place. After a happy reunion, Mary introduced the girls to Mr. Griffith, and he hired them both on the spot.

Ever since Carl Laemmle at IMP had touted Mary as "America's Greatest Film Star," the public had been able to attach a name to the famous face. Now, Mary's name began to appear on the posters and handbills at Biograph, although not yet on the films themselves. Biograph was sticking to the old, unspoken agreement about actor anonymity.

But things for Mary were not the same at Biograph now. Upon her return, Mary discovered that other young girls had taken her place in the company. She was no longer the only choice Griffith had when he wanted someone to play the ingenue. Certainly, both Lillian and Dorothy Gish could fill the bill. There was great rivalry among the actresses now. It often seemed to Mary as if she were getting the parts no one else wanted.

Her failing marriage and her disillusionment over what she saw as unfair treatment by Mr. Griffith contributed to Mary's general feeling of unhappiness. She and Owen Moore separated several times between 1912 and 1916. Owen cited Charlotte's interference in their marriage as one of the main reasons for their troubles. For her part, Mary suffered through Owen's long bouts of silence and his hostility toward Charlotte. She longed to go back to the stage, thinking this might be what she needed.

When Mary finally shared these thoughts with Mr. Griffith, he scoffed at the idea, saying no self-respecting theatrical producer would hire her now, after she'd had three years in the flickers.

When Griffith gave the lead in *The Sands of Dee* to Mae Marsh, an inexperienced shop girl he'd only just hired from her job in a department store, Mary was hurt and angry. Perhaps Griffith, too, was feeling disillusioned.

In May 1912, they argued over the issue of Mary baring her legs for a role in *Man's Genesis*. The lead, which Griffith had offered Mary, was expected to wear a grass skirt in the film. Mary refused.

"In those days," she later explained, "we even wore stockings and shoes in bathing!" Griffith gave the part to someone else, and Mary decided it was time to make good on her intention to return to the theatre.

She called David Belasco and invited him to a screening of her latest comedy, *Lena and the Geese*. After seeing the film, Belasco had high praise for Mary's performance. Better yet, he offered her the leading role as a blind girl, Juliet, in a play he was about to produce called *A Good Little Devil*. Rehearsals were to start in three days.

Elated, Mary bounded back to the Biograph studio, where she told Mr. Griffith about Belasco's offer. There had been no written contract between Griffith and Mary, and she was legally free to go. They made good use of the three days prior to her leaving by making one last picture together.

That film was *The New York Hat*, by screenwriter Anita Loos. It was released December 15, 1912. Her co-star was Lionel

Barrymore, and Lillian Gish and Jack Pickford had minor roles. With its many close-ups of Mary, it was one of the best short movies she'd ever made at Biograph.

Mary and Mr. Griffith parted on good terms, with him wishing her well. "I suddenly realized," she later wrote, "how much I would miss my beloved Biograph and the guiding hand of this brilliant man."

Initially, Mary felt nervous about having to say lines again, after three years away from live theatre. It turned out that she had nothing to fear. However, she did find playing blind Juliet in *A Good Little Devil* very demanding.

Playing a blind girl, on stage, Mary had to avoid ever looking directly into anyone's face. Instead, she had to stare into the space above their heads. She later described the constant staring as "the most exhausting strain" of her entire career, both on stage and screen. When she left the theatre after each performance, her whole body — every nerve, bone, and muscle — was aching.

The play opened first in Philadelphia, and D.W. Griffith and the entire Biograph company were there in the front row when the curtain rose. The Broadway opening was at the Republic Theatre on January 8, 1913. Hundreds of fans of Mary's silent

Mary in The New York Hat *(1912). This was to be her last Biograph picture.*

movies came out to see "Little Mary" live. The play ran for several months and garnered rave reviews from the critics. By the time it closed, *A Good Little Devil* had played for 152 performances.

But it had not provided Mary with the satisfaction she had hoped for. Being used to shooting outdoors on location, she now found the stage sets in the theatre flat and uninteresting. As she later described it, she missed "the novelty, the adventure from day to day into unknown areas of pantomime and photography." She was made for motion pictures. She knew she had to go back.

6

Her Name in Lights

The Europeans were already producing feature-length movies — films that ran for an hour or more — and these were starting to show up in theatres in the U.S. The Americans countered with Adolph Zukor.

Zukor, the Hungarian-born producer, former furrier, and nickelodeon owner, had developed a concept that he called "Famous Players in Famous Plays." His idea was to make feature-length films of four or five reels that would star well-known actors from the stage in the roles for which they were famous. He hoped these longer films would serve to attract more of the middle class to the movies.

Zukor and his partner, Daniel Frohman, bought the screen rights to *A Good Little Devil*, which included its New York cast. Mary Pickford saw this as an opportunity to get back into the motion pictures she loved, without sacrificing her theatrical art.

But rather than being what Mary had expected — a film version of the play, using action and pantomime — Zukor's *A Good Little Devil* was a silent reproduction. The actors had to read their entire parts in front of the camera, despite the fact these words would never be heard, while David Belasco was filmed sitting by a fireplace, visualizing the play. Mary called it "a monumental failure."

Fortunately, all was not lost. Famous Players offered Mary Pickford a one-year contract for three back-to-back movies at a salary of $500 a week. It was more money than many Americans were making in a year.

The first feature was *In the Bishop's Carriage*, released in 1913. It was not the religious film that Mary's Methodist grandmother had thought it to be. Mary played a thief in the movie, and in one scene she revealed her legs in a ballet costume. It was the first and the last of Mary's pictures that Grandma Smith would ever go to see.

Away from the camera, Mary dressed modestly. She never drank alcohol in public or handled anything that might be mistaken for a cigarette. Her long hair was worn up, a fashion dictated for women by polite society in 1913. In spite of her wealth, she and her mother lived simple lives; most of Mary's salary was invested or put into the bank.

Caprice was Mary's second film of 1913. She played a mountain girl in the picture, and Owen Moore's appearance as her city boyfriend may have been a concession made to her by Zukor. Mary was developing her trademark film persona — the spirited, independent young woman filled with fiery determination.

Several times Mary and Owen had tried to get back together, but it had never lasted. Mary seemed unable to separate herself from Charlotte, and this situation only made Owen's drinking worse.

When *Caprice* was finished, and with Mary recuperating from an emergency appendectomy, she, Charlotte, and Edwin S. Porter, vice-president of Famous Players, went to Los Angeles to set up the company's West Coast offices. Other movie troupes had already arrived, and Hollywood was starting to fill up with wooden stages.

Mary had read a story in a magazine that she particularly liked, and she told Zukor that she thought it would make a good movie. Although she couldn't remember which magazine it came from (and it didn't seem to matter), Zukor paid her $100 to turn it into a screenplay. *Hearts Adrift*, released in February 1914, was Famous Players's first West Coast production.

Mary loved Mr. Zukor and his old-world dignity and charm. She called him "Papa Zukor," and he treated her like one of his own children. Mary would stay with Zukor's company for five and a half years, and she always referred to that time as the happiest years of her screen life. Later, she wrote, "... to the end of our association he was a loving devoted father."

Mary was back in New York to renegotiate her salary, when late one afternoon, Mr. Zukor invited her to have tea with him in a restaurant. The restaurant was across the street from the theatre where *Hearts Adrift* was playing.

As much as Mary enjoyed sipping tea and chatting with Papa Zukor that afternoon, she did wonder why the man seemed to be dawdling. They were still at the table when darkness fell. It was at that point that Mr. Zukor revealed the reason for his invitation: across the street, on the theatre marquee overlooking Broadway, blazing in electric lights, was Mary's name. Mary called it "one of the most thrilling sights" of her whole career. She almost felt sorry she'd asked the dear man to raise her salary to $1,000 a week while he was planning this wonderful surprise for her.

In order to finance Mary's next picture, it was said that Zukor had to borrow on his life insurance and hawk Mrs. Zukor's diamond necklace. But this was to be the movie that would save his company from bankruptcy, and it was the most successful picture of Mary's career thus far.

The film was *Tess of the Storm Country*, an eighty-minute feature, with Mary playing her most violent role to date. The is the story of a young girl who leads a squatters' revolt against a group of corrupt landowners.

The role was perfect for Mary, and her performance was brilliant. She would later refer to *Tess* as the real beginning of her career in motion pictures. It was Mary's fifth feature film, and the first of those which are still in existence today.

For the opening of *Tess* in San Francisco, David "Pop" Grauman put the following on his theatre's marquee:

Tess of the Storm Country
Mary Pickford
America's Sweetheart

Mary had received the nickname by which she would be known for all the years to come.

Famous Players owed its ability to make a picture of this size with its small West Coast staff to the fact that everyone did more than his assigned job. Edwin S. Porter, vice-president of Famous Players, was also the cameraman, the cameraman's assistant, the director, the producer, and the head electrician. Mary and Charlotte even pitched in and used their own belongings as props.

There was one problem with making movies out in Hollywood. Because the negatives had to be sent back east to be developed, the company didn't get to see the dailies — all the shots from the day before. Dailies always helped to determine the mood of the picture and then to maintain that mood throughout. *Tess* had been edited and released without any of the West Coast company ever seeing it. They were all greatly relieved that it was such a hit in New York.

Pickford and Harold Lockwood in Tess of the Storm Country *(1914).*

Tess of the Storm Country established Adolph Zukor as a major producer and Mary Pickford as the first lady of the movies. The movie played on four continents and raised Mary to a level of stardom never before seen, giving birth to the star system of the American movie industry.

In November 1914, Zukor raised Mary's salary to $2,000 a week.

The characters Mary played in her films — working class or slum girls, seemed to mirror her own real-life beginnings. She often portrayed the plucky tomboy type, someone as capable as Mary was herself of handling any trouble that came her way.

She was able to get jobs at Famous Players for Lottie and Jack, as well as for Owen Moore, and when she starred in *Cinderella* in 1914, Owen played Prince Charming. He appeared with her again in *Mistress Nell*. Both films, directed by Mary's friend James Kirkwood, who had been hired by Zukor to direct nine of Mary's pictures, were filmed in New York, where Owen and Mary were again trying to live together.

According to James Kirkwood Jr., his father and Mary Pickford had once been lovers and had even hoped to marry one day. But it seems unlikely that Kirkwood, who was simultaneously directing Mary and Owen Moore, would be carrying on an affair with the wife of the volatile actor. Kirkwood would have heard the ugly stories, like the one actress Madge Bellamy swore came straight from Charlotte, that Moore had taken a whip to Mary.

In 1914 Zukor put Broadway's Marguerite Clark, a girl even tinier than Mary, under contract. Mary saw this as Zukor developing another "Mary" type and she resented it. Soon after, the dual roles in *The Prince and the Pauper*, which Mary had wanted, went to Clark. Feeling threatened, Mary requested (and received) twice her previous salary and one half the profits of her films.

In *Fanchon the Cricket*, released May 10, 1915, Mary plays a wild girl who lives in the woods with her crazy grandmother; this is a film from a scenario by Frances Marion and was directed by James Kirkwood. It was the only full-length feature where all three Pickfords appeared together. Sources do not agree whether or not Fred Astaire and his sister, Adele, also appeared in the picture.

After the success of *Tess*, Zukor had Mary make seven features in 1914 and eight in 1915. He had realized that he could sell all his pictures on the strength of Mary's performances.

One day in 1915, Mary noticed the large crowd lining up at the box office to see *Rags*, one of her very successful pictures. Later, when the same theatre was showing another Famous Players film, she saw that the place was almost deserted.

When she asked Zukor about this, she learned that Paramount, who distributed Famous Players films, was renting the company's movies through a system called "block booking." If a theatre wanted to show Mary's pictures, it had no choice but to take a package that included other lesser movies. Mary's name was being used to make money on movies unable to make it on their own.

When contract time rolled around again, she would insist that her pictures be sold separately, not packaged with other Famous Players films.

Every company in the business was now making fantastic offers to Mary Pickford. Universal Studios, formerly Carl Laemmle's Independent Motion Picture Company (IMP), tried unsuccessfully to entice her away from Famous Players. Universal had all thirty-three of her old IMP films, however, and in the summer of 1914 it re-released them, much to Mary's displeasure.

One of the other film companies, Mutual, home to famous comedian Charlie Chaplin, offered Mary $1 million to sign with them. She took that information to Papa Zukor. He refused to meet it but offered her a voice in choosing her films and a guarantee of $10,000 a week. Mary accepted Zukor's offer.

On June 16, 1916, Zukor's Famous Players merged with the Jesse L. Lasky Feature Play Company. Other principals in the new Famous Players-Lasky, the largest motion picture company in the world, were Samuel Goldfish (Lasky's brother-in-law; he later changed his surname to Goldwyn) and Cecil B. DeMille. Both Zukor and Lasky released their films through Paramount, and their combined shares enabled them to take control of that company.

Famous Players had asked Mary to delay signing her new contract until after the merger and promised her a sizable sum if she would do so. Later, she tried to see Zukor to remind him of his promise. Instead, Samuel Goldfish intervened. Mary was furious. She had been put under contract by Zukor, she said, and refused to discuss the matter with Goldfish.

Mary hated the merger and never believed that Zukor had encouraged it. What had once been an intimate family group was now, according to Mary, a huge machine, cold and impersonal.

Her first picture with Famous Players-Lasky was *Less Than the Dust*, released in November 1916. Mary called it her worst picture ever. In it, she plays a Hindustani slave girl, and Mary blamed the picture's failure on interference from Famous Players-Lasky.

The outspoken Sam Goldfish had been openly critical of stage mothers of Charlotte's ilk, and Mary and Goldfish developed a mutual dislike of each other. About their relationship, Mary later wrote, "While I do not care to do business with him,

I must be frank in my recognition of those qualities of his that have gone toward helping to build the industry."

Goldwyn said of Mary that it took longer to negotiate one of her famous contracts than it did for her to make a picture.

When Mary signed her new two-year contract on June 24, 1916, she became the first movie actress to produce her own work. She would have approval over the directors and other actors hired for her pictures.

Under the new contract, Mary would be required to make no more than six films a year, so that more care could be taken in making them. Fewer films would also create greater demand for them.

Zukor, as the most powerful in the conglomerate, would negotiate all of Mary's contracts. Her films would be distributed through Artcraft, a special distribution branch of Famous Players-Lasky-Paramount. Most significant was the fact that Artcraft did not "block book."

Zukor agreed to pay Mary half a million dollars a year or half the net profits of her films, whichever amount was greater. There was also a bonus of $300,000 and $10,000 a week for the four weeks it had taken her and Charlotte to negotiate the contract. Special perks included a press agent, a secretary, a private studio in New York, and train travel in a parlour coach to the West Coast for wintertime shoots.

The press announced that Mary Pickford was now the highest paid woman in the world. She was making more than the American president. Mary set her family up in a fine New York apartment and bought herself a new caramel-coloured Cadillac. It was her first real indulgence.

The Pickford Film Corporation, Mary's own production unit, with Charlotte as treasurer, was set up within the framework of the Famous Players organization. Rather than being her boss, Zukor was now her partner. Mary had achieved creative freedom and for the next four years would make her best pictures.

Financially, Mary was at the peak of her career, but as if she were still that small child riding the trains during her barnstorming days, she continued to worry about her family's security.

Meanwhile, back in Toronto, tours of the city began to include her birthplace, the humble brick row house on University Avenue.

7

Enter Douglas Fairbanks

Back in 1913, Adolph Zukor had invited Broadway actor Douglas Fairbanks to be one of his original famous players. Like most actors on the stage, Fairbanks didn't think very highly of the movie business, and he turned the invitation down.

Born Douglas Ulman in 1883 in Denver, Colorado, Douglas had been a mischievous youngster, a daredevil who was forever climbing trees and frightening his poor mother by walking along the edge of their roof.

His mother, Ella, had four sons from three different husbands. Douglas's only full brother was Robert, who was two years his senior. The boys also had an older half-brother, John. The family had lost touch with the fourth brother, whose name was Norris. After Ella's third husband, Charles Ulman (an alcoholic), deserted them, she and the boys took the name of Fairbanks from her deceased first husband, her one true love.

By the time Douglas had finished high school, he'd decided that he wanted to be an actor. He was lucky enough to get a job in the theatre and from there seemed to have little trouble establishing himself on Broadway. He played in a string of comedies and had his first real success in 1906 in *The Man of the Hour*. Eventually, he became one of Broadway's most popular matinee idols, known for his infectious grin and his feats of daring. Full of energy, Douglas Fairbanks was always on the move, never walking if he could run, vaulting over anything in his path.

Fairbanks also had a reputation as a ladies' man, but his wife, Beth, the daughter of a wealthy cotton tycoon, was either unaware of it or simply chose to ignore the fact. No woman of her social status would do otherwise.

Although she'd seen him before, Mary Pickford did not officially meet Douglas Fairbanks until they were both invited to a get-together in November 1915. Mary's latest picture, *A Girl of Yesterday*, had been released the month before. It was the first time Mary had ever flown, and with this picture, she became the first actress ever to fly in a film (with a pilot, of course).

The script of the film, in which Mary and her brother Jack played sibling orphans, called for the villain in the movie to abduct Mary in an airplane. Stunt pilot Glenn Martin, who would later found his own aviation company, was hired to fly the plane.

Only a dozen years separate the making of this film and the Wright brothers' first flight at Kitty Hawk. In spite of Martin's skill as a pilot, Charlotte feared for Mary's safety. She would allow the sequence to be filmed, providing the plane never got more than 100 feet off the ground. Director Allan Dwan knew it was far more dangerous to fly a plane that close to the ground than it was at 10,000 feet, but Charlotte's word, when it came to Mary's well-being, was law.

Dwan managed to sidestep Charlotte's orders by having Martin fly the plane parallel to a road on top of the Griffith Park mountains, with the camera car following it around the contour of the mountain. Although the plane was far above ground level, it was never more than 100 feet from the ground atop the mountain.

At one point during the airplane sequence, the stunt pilot turned to the movie villain and said, "Look, I don't even have to hold on." The already-nervous actor fainted. Director Dwan saw the villain flop over and witnessed Mary trying to prop him up, shaking him frantically.

The November gathering was held at Tarrytown, New York, at the mansion of Elsie Janis, a musical comedy star, and the girl whose mother Charlotte had pumped back in Toronto for advice on how to get her own daughter noticed. Among the invited guests were Mary Pickford, Douglas Fairbanks, and their respective spouses. Mary and Owen were temporarily back together.

Initially, Mary was not a fan of the swarthy-complexioned Fairbanks. "I didn't think much of him at first," she said later. "He was too exuberant. And," she added, "I was a Canadian," as if that explained her reticence. She had by then seen Fairbanks on Broadway in *A Gentleman of Leisure* and knew he was starting to appear in movies.

When Elsie Janis suggested they all take a walk outside that afternoon, Owen and Douglas immediately joined her. It was a cold, drizzly day in mid-November, and Mary and Beth, both of whom were less than enthusiastic, trailed behind. Before they'd gone very far, Beth gave up and returned to the house.

Mary caught up with the others at a stream they'd just crossed. She was reluctant to step onto the log that lay over the icy water for fear of ruining her expensive new shoes. The rest of the group was waiting for her on the other side.

Suddenly, Douglas jumped back across to Mary's side, swept her up in his arms, and carried her over the brook. Mary later wrote that she didn't see anything romantic about this action. It was just Douglas being Douglas. It was the way he would respond to any "lady in distress."

Mary and Doug met again about a month later. She was living at the Knickerbocker Hotel in New York, and Douglas was at the Algonquin, where his close friend, Frank Case, was the proprietor. Case was giving a dance one night, and he invited Mary.

Douglas Fairbanks was there with Beth, but it was Mary with whom he spent most of the evening, dancing. Between dances, they sat in the lobby and talked about the movie business they both loved.

Douglas was very complimentary about Mary's mastery of the art of pantomime, putting her on the same level as Charlie Chaplin. "You do less apparent acting than anyone else I know," he said. "Because of this, you express more."

Mary was thrilled. She'd never heard anything like that from Owen, who was more likely to belittle her work if he had anything to say about it at all. "I hugged the echo of his words for days," Mary later wrote, "repeating them over and over again to myself. I had been living in half shadows, and now a brilliant light was suddenly cast upon me, the sunlight of Douglas's approval and admiration."

Mary had reached the unhappy point in her personal life where she was trying not to think about her less than ideal marriage. She had made her choices, and believed she had to live with them. She certainly never thought she'd ever fall in love again. "I was convinced that a happy marriage was a schoolgirl illusion," she wrote.

Within a few days, Douglas invited Mary and Charlotte to meet his mother, Ella, in her New York apartment, and the two older women became friends. He also took Mary to meet his young son, six-year-old Douglas Jr.

Neither Doug nor Mary seemed to realize they were falling in love, but over the next little while, both Charlotte and Ella became aware of the growing attraction between the couple. The mothers could see trouble ahead.

Triangle Films Corporation, based in California, was a new organization formed in 1915 by the Big Three in motion pictures — Thomas Ince, formerly of IMP; Mack Sennett, founder of Keystone Studio; and D.W. Griffith, who had left Biograph shortly after Mary. To compete with Famous Players in Famous Plays, Triangle hired over sixty stage actors, some of them with salaries as high as $4,000 a week. Triangle's mandate was to release films at prices the average movie-goer could afford. Douglas Fairbanks had signed with the company in the spring of 1915.

Fairbanks's first film with Triangle was called *The Lamb*. He made eleven films in 1916, all but one of them feature-length. By late 1916, Douglas Fairbanks was one of the top three film stars in America, not far behind his good friend Charlie Chaplin. In the number one spot was Mary Pickford.

Although Adolph Zukor made most of his movies in New York, other companies in the industry were quickly moving to the West Coast. Hollywood was filling up with big, barn-like studios, and becoming populated by producers, directors, executives, stars, and wannabe stars. Every day, the L.A. newspapers carried advertisements for extras to play in crowd scenes. Tourists, too, began to show up to watch the films being made and were most eager to search out the movie stars.

Douglas Fairbanks went to California in 1916, rented a big house in Beverly Hills, and had his wife, Beth, and young Douglas Jr. join him from New York. Fairbanks was turning out a film nearly every month now, and he grew rich, receiving a share of the profit from his pictures.

Early in 1917, Fairbanks left Triangle and joined Famous Players-Lasky. He established his own production unit within the company and released his films though Artcraft-Paramount. Most of the pictures were melodramas enhanced by his famous acrobatics.

Mary was in New York in 1916 when Douglas came back east for Ella Fairbanks's funeral. Having been fond of Douglas's mother, Mary wrote him a note expressing her sympathy, and Douglas asked to see her. They went for a drive together.

Mrs. Fairbanks had always been superstitious when it came to clocks, and when Mary noticed that the dashboard clock in the car had stopped at the exact hour of Ella's death, she and Douglas decided it was a sign from his mother. They took the sign to mean that Ella was with them in spirit and was giving their burgeoning relationship her blessing. Ever after, Mary and Doug used the phrase "by the clock" to signify promises between them that could not be broken.

Maurice Tourneau, who had come to New York from Paris in 1914, directed Mary in the 1916 film *The Pride of the Clan*. The movie was shot on location at Marblehead, Massachusetts, a setting so much like the coast of Scotland, with seabirds flying about and waves crashing onto the rocks, that one could easily imagine the picture had been filmed in that country.

In the film's climax, Mary's character is aboard a fishing boat that is supposedly sinking. The situation got a little too authentic, however, and suddenly the director shouted, "Everybody leave the boat! We're sinking!"

They actually were. As the scene was being shot, some barrels that were on the deck had shifted, and gradually the boat began to fill with water. Immediately, the whole cast and crew went over the side, where some were lowered into a lifeboat and others swam the 300 yards to shore. No one seemed to have noticed that Mary was not among them.

She had been using the cabin of the boat as her dressing room and now remembered that she'd left her cosmetic kit inside. She headed back to get it.

Just as she was about to open the door to the cabin, something told her not to, some instinct which she referred to in her memoirs as "a voice." She turned and hurried back toward the side of the boat, surprising director Tourneau, who thought he was the last one on board and was about to abandon ship. By this time, the water was up to their knees, and the cabin would surely have been completely submerged.

Fortunately, Tourneau was able to help Mary into the lifeboat before swimming to shore himself. Mary credits that mysterious voice inside her head with saving her life, and she continued to be guided by it over the years.

She had had an earlier brush with death when she was filming *In the Sultan's Garden* for IMP in 1911, and it, too, had involved an incident on the water.

The scene they were shooting called for Mary's character to have been sewn into a bag and tossed into the Bosphorus (actually, the Hudson River). The lady-in-waiting in the story had given the girl a dagger beforehand, and she would use this to cut herself free of the bag. Subsequently, Mary's character would be rescued by her American admirer, in a speedboat.

Mary couldn't swim, and she was instructed to tread water, looking as if she'd just cut herself out of the bag, until she could be rescued. The operator of the speedboat was so excited about being in a movie for the first time that he wasn't paying attention. Suddenly, it became clear to the crew on the dock that the boat was heading straight for Mary, who was bobbing in the water.

Realizing what was about to happen, one of the men who had been told to keep an eye on her dived into the river, grabbing Mary by the legs and pulling her under, just as the speedboat passed overhead. Panic-stricken, Mary didn't know what was happening and was convinced that her rescuer was trying to drown her.

Everyone on the dock, including Charlotte, watched in horror until finally Mary came to the surface. She was barely conscious.

Mary had often played characters of other nationalities. She was an Inuit girl in *Little Pal*, released July 1, 1915; a Japanese girl in *Madame Butterfly*, released November 8, 1915; a Dutch girl in *Hulda from Holland*, released in July 1916; an Indian girl in *Less than the Dust*; and now, in *The Pride of the Clan*, a Scottish girl. But box office sales always seemed to slump whenever she moved away from the crowd-pleasing "Little Mary" roles.

Frances Marion adapted Mary's next picture, *The Poor Little Rich Girl*, from a stage play. This movie would be the first time Mary starred as a little girl throughout an entire film. It was bound to please her fans.

Frances Marion, a journalist and a combat correspondent during the First World War, has been credited with being the most renowned female screenwriter of the twentieth century. She was a close friend of Mary's, becoming her official screenwriter and also appearing in some early Pickford films.

The two young women were so in tune with each other that together they wrote magazine articles, under Mary's name, for *Ladies' Home Journal* and *Pictorial Review*, as well as a newspaper column that ran in 1916 and 1917, where Mary answered questions and discussed her life and her movies. Mary became the first film actress to appear on the cover of a national magazine, and in 1917 the readers of *Woman's Home Companion* voted Mary Pickford "The Ideal American Woman."

Released in March 1917, *The Poor Little Rich Girl* features Mary playing a wealthy eleven-year-old who longs for a normal life. Mary appears shorter in the film than she actually was, because director Tourneau used furniture that was two-thirds larger than usual, so that Mary has to scramble up to sit in a chair.

Mary believed that you had to study people around you in order to make a character real and believable. "I didn't act," she explained. "I *was* the character. I lived the character." She knew how to re-create a child. She'd observed how a child walks, how a small child gets up off the floor — bottom first. She had studied the way a child's face reacts to different emotions, how a child stands with her toes pointed slightly inward.

Mary and Frances Marion decided that what their picture needed was some humour, and they added some unscripted slapstick, which included a hilarious mud fight. Director Tourneau was not happy; he wanted *The Poor Little Rich Girl* to be a dignified picture. Mary controlled the finished product, however, and Tourneau gave up. It appears that Zukor, too, let

Mary have her way with the film, although she'd barred Lasky's people from the set.

The end result was a movie quite different from the original stage play and script. When the studio execs saw the finished product, they were appalled. Mary was summoned to Adolph Zukor's office and told that, as a consequence, her next two pictures would be directed by Cecil B. DeMille. DeMille's word, as part of the merger agreement, was law. Not Pickford's.

Mary was genuinely sorry she'd let Papa Zukor down and agreed to send DeMille a telegram in which she promised to obey him without question. Both she and Frances Marion went home in tears, convinced they'd ruined the picture.

In the spring of 1917, Zukor sent Mary and her entire family to California. The entourage included Lottie and her baby, Mary Pickford Rupp. The child's name would later be changed to Gwynne.

Mary had to make her two pictures for DeMille in Los Angeles but would end up staying permanently. She and Charlotte settled into a bungalow in Los Angeles, and when Owen begged to be given another chance, Mary relented and let him move in.

Lottie Pickford had accepted an offer from American Film Company in Santa Barbara as a star in a serial. Unfortunately, she became involved with alcohol and drugs, as did younger brother Jack. Mary would spend years paying to get Jack out of trouble, even producing pictures for him to keep him in work. But he went from one scrape to the next, always confident that Mary or Charlotte would step in and save him.

Mary's first film with DeMille was *A Romance of the Redwoods*, released in May 1917. She lived up to her agreement and managed to keep all her bright ideas for the picture to herself.

In a review of *A Romance of the Redwoods*, Vachel Lindsay, poet and film critic for *The New Republic*, said, "If there is anything in a film at all, it is worth seeing three times. I went to see this one six times because I was glad Mary was beginning to emerge."

In the meantime, Mary and Frances Marion went to see the New York premiere of *The Poor Little Rich Girl*, which was now re-cut. To her surprise, Mary was mobbed by enthusiastic fans at the theatre. In spite of her fears, the picture was a smash hit. Even Papa Zukor sent her a congratulatory telegram.

The Poor Little Rich Girl turned out to be one of the most beloved of all Mary's films. Several close-ups in the picture were illuminated using a Pickford innovation — a "baby spotlight" that was situated at a low level to provided artificial light to Mary's face. She had discovered the technique purely by accident one day at her dressing table.

When Douglas Fairbanks joined Famous Players-Lasky, it was inevitable that he and Mary would run into each other at the studio. It was hard to deny the attraction between them, harder still for either to resist it. Because they were both married to other people, they began to meet in secret, either at Mary's bungalow or at a cottage in Laurel Canyon owned by Douglas's brother, Robert.

Owen Moore had begun to drink heavily again, and Mary told him to leave, this time for good. The surly Owen demanded to know the truth about the rumours he'd been hearing, and when Mary told him, he threatened violence again Douglas. Judiciously, Fairbanks decided this might be the perfect time to go elsewhere to make his next picture.

Mary's second DeMille picture was *The Little American*. Full of anti-German sentiment, it was released July 2, 1917. The film was based on the actual sinking of the liner *Lusitania*, which had been torpedoed by a German submarine on May 7, 1915. The liner sank in less than eighteen minutes and 1,198 lives were lost with it.

In the film, Mary's character is aboard the liner *Veritania*, en route to France, when it is similarly torpedoed. Following her rescue, she is held captive by German soldiers. Critics said *The Little American* was so realistic that it seemed more like a newsreel than a movie.

From their earliest days together with David Belasco in *The Warrens of Virginia*, Cecil B. DeMille had respected Mary's dedication to her work. It didn't hurt that he made more money on *A Romance of the Redwoods* and *The Little American* with Mary Pickford than he had for any of his previous films.

When the U.S. finally entered the war in the spring of 1917, Mary threw herself behind the war effort. She posed for pro-war posters, started a tobacco fund for the soldiers, and sent pictures of herself to decorate the trenches on the battlefield. She adopted the second battalion of the First California Field Artillery and became its honorary colonel. A frequent visitor to Camp Kearney, near San Diego, she presented each of the 600 recruits there with a gold locket containing her picture, and the young men were wearing them when they shipped out to France.

As well as personally purchasing American Liberty Bonds, Mary bought thousands of dollars in subscriptions to the Canadian War Loan and made a point of delivering the money to Toronto in person.

The secretary of the U.S. Treasury, William McAdoo, asked Mary Pickford and Douglas Fairbanks to join Charlie Chaplin on a tour to promote and sell Liberty Bonds. The drive began in April 1918, in Washington. Huge crowds came out to see the stars of Hollywood, with Cobourg, Ontario, native comedienne Marie Dressler representing Broadway, as they paraded down Pennsylvania Avenue.

Thousands more came out to hear them at a rally on Wall Street in New York City where they made anti-German speeches. Barely able to lift the heavy megaphone, Mary didn't disappoint the crowd, as she was wearing her trademark long curls loose down her back. Charlie Chaplin did his "Little Tramp" routine, twirling his walking stick, and Douglas Fairbanks flashed his infectious grin and performed his famous acrobatics for everyone. It was the first time Hollywood and the government in

Douglas Fairbanks, Mary Pickford, and Charlie Chaplin, circa 1917. Here, the trio are plotting appearances to sell war bonds.

Washington had worked together. It was also the first time Mary Pickford and Douglas Fairbanks had appeared side-by-side in public.

As their relationship developed, Douglas was bothered by the fact that he couldn't warm up to Mary's family. The Pickfords were a source of concern for him, particularly the fact that most of them drank. Fairbanks himself was a teetotaler, having promised his mother that he would not touch alcohol until after the age of forty.

Douglas wished Mary's mother were more refined, more like his own mother had been. Charlotte had been drinking for years, often trying to hide it from Mary, and now that Charlotte's figure had become barrel-like, she reminded Douglas of a low-class washerwoman.

Lottie Pickford, the forgotten daughter who had always lived in Mary's shadow, had become a rebel. Once her baby daughter was born, she returned to her irresponsible lifestyle, drinking, using drugs, and throwing noisy all-night parties.

Prior to 1920, Mary's brother, Jack, managed to make almost thirty movies, but he was unpredictable and a heavy drinker. He could be charming when it suited him, and for most of his life he lived off rich women. It was all a bit too much for someone like Douglas, who felt he had certain standards to maintain.

For her part, Mary was not especially fond of Doug's friend, Charlie Chaplin. She found the man to be moody and intro-verted. At other times, Chaplin could bore her by lecturing her on his left-wing beliefs. What's more, he and Douglas used to set up elaborate pranks together, which Mary found juvenile and annoying.

But Mary and Chaplin both loved Douglas and so they toler-ated each other for his sake. And after all, their fans expected this trio of top stars to love one another. For ten years, Mary grudgingly took part in the crazy antics that became a trademark of the three.

As soon as Mary was released from her obligation to DeMille, she asked Frances Marion to adapt for the screen *Rebecca of Sunnybrook Farm*, a book by Kate Douglas Wiggin, published in 1903. She chose her former co-star Marshall "Mickey" Neilan (*Rags, A Girl of Yesterday, Madame Butterfly*, all from 1915) to direct the picture. It was released September 22, 1917.

"I was twenty-two years old [she was actually closer to twenty-five] when I played that unforgettable little eleven-year-old from Sunnybrook Farm," Mary later wrote. "But I enjoyed the part as if I were still a child myself."

"It was inevitable that one of the most popular child heroines in recent fiction should be portrayed on the screen by the most popular film ingenue," raved the *New York Dramatic Mirror* when *Rebecca* was released.

Director Neilan, an Irishman, could always be counted on to make Mary laugh. "Mickey was one of the most delightful, aggravating, gifted and charming human beings I have ever known," Mary said. "To my way of thinking he was the best director ever, better than the great D.W. Griffith."

The next picture, *The Little Princess*, was released November 7, 1917, with Neilan again directing and with Charles Rosher as cameraman. Rosher gave this film and *A Poor Little Rich Girl* a fairy-tale quality with his lighting techniques, and he became Mary's favourite cameraman.

Stella Maris, released July 21, 1918, was Mary's third film with Neilan as director. She was quite capable of directing her own pictures and had to occasionally when Neilan fell off the wagon. But Mickey was the best, and she trusted him.

Mary plays the title role in the film: the beautiful, sheltered invalid, Stella. But she also plays the unlikely part of Unity Blake, a homely little Cockney household slave. Mary is totally unrecognizable in the role. She plastered her hair down with Vaseline, applied special makeup around her eyes so that they appeared smaller, and made her cheeks look hollow and her nostrils appear wider. She also darkened her teeth.

D.W. Griffith used to say that Mary could never play anyone who was ugly, but with this picture she proved him wrong.

When Papa Zukor saw Mary in this unbecoming disguise, he was appalled, convinced the film would be a disaster. Mary was quick to assure him that she was also playing a second character, one he'd approve of — the beautiful Stella, with her full array of long curls. *Stella Maris* is today considered one of Mary Pickford's finest films.

After *Stella Maris*, Mary made five more films for Zukor: *Amarilly of Clothes-Line Alley, M'Liss, How Could You, Jean? Johanna Enlists*, and *Captain Kidd, Jr.* And for most of them, she played the slightly scruffy teenager.

Mary was getting tired of having to play the "girl with the golden curls." But she didn't want to offend all the little girls who loved her. At one point, she had eighteen false ringlets made up, at $50 a piece, for those days when the humidity made her own curls go limp.

Those long ringlets, which she often referred to as "a miserable nuisance," took Mary an hour to twirl into shape around her finger each day, and they meant having to sleep with three different sized rollers in her hair every night.

"I hate curls," she is quoted as saying. "I loathe them!"

* * *

Back in 1917, two exhibitors, Thomas Tally and J.D. Williams, had set up First National, a distribution company that would eliminate the middleman by making and showing their own productions. Looking for stars for the new company, they had already signed up Charlie Chaplin, and they offered Mary $675,000 for three pictures and one-half of the profits, plus $50,000 to Charlotte for her services. Included was one clause that was particularly important to Mary: no block booking.

She was close to the end of her two-year contract with Zukor and his Famous Players-Lasky. She asked him if he would match First National's offer. Regretfully, he refused, and Mary knew it was over between them. Although they had become physically distant, with Zukor still working from the New York office and Mary making movies in California, they parted dear friends, bidding each other tearful goodbyes.

Zukor went on to pursue his own dream of establishing a chain of theatres across the country. Years later, when Mary and Papa Zukor were entering the lobby of the Paramount Theatre in New York together, he told her that her pictures were what had made that building possible.

Charlotte had gone to New York and bought the screen rights to the novels *Pollyanna* and *Daddy Long Legs* for Mary. The latter became Mary's first picture with First National. It was directed by Marshall Neilan, who also played the suitor in the film. Grossing $1.3 million, it was Mary's biggest financial success up to that point, and it became one of the best-loved of all her pictures.

In November 1918, Mary and Charlotte set up the Mary Pickford Company, a fifty-fifty deal between them, with Charlotte looking after the business end. For five and a half years under Zukor, Mary had been able to choose her director and co-stars, but she had been a producer in name only. That was all Zukor ever allowed. Now, for the first time, she had total control.

Mary's contract with First National was for three pictures in three months, and production was to begin December 1, 1918.

Around this time, rumours began to circulate about a possible merger between several of the top companies in the movie industry, including First National and Zukor's Famous Players-Lasky-Paramount, in an effort to try to control salaries. If this were to happen, it could mean only two or three large studios remaining in America, greatly limiting the stars' bargaining power.

Under First National, Mary and Charlie Chaplin were sharing their profits with the company. Why not, they asked each other, become their own distributors?

On April 17, 1919, Mary Pickford, Charlie Chaplin, Douglas Fairbanks, D.W. Griffith, and William S. Hart formed United Artists, a company owned and operated by the leading lights in the motion picture business, known as "The Big Five."

Many insiders were of the opinion that people as flighty and unpredictable as movie stars couldn't possibly make a success of such a venture. In fact, someone quipped, "Now the lunatics have taken over the asylum."

William S. Hart was soon lured away by Zukor, but each of the four remaining partners invested $100,000 and pledged to meet a quota of movies for United Artists. Mary's quota was for three pictures in three years. All of the partners, with the exception of Fairbanks, whose contract with Famous Players had already expired, had earlier commitments to fulfill. Mary and Chaplin both owed films to First National, and Griffith was working on two pictures for Paramount.

Mary completed her commitment to First National with *The Hoodlum*, released September 1, 1919 (in spite of being struck by the 1918 influenza epidemic and being off sick for four weeks), and *Heart o' the Hills*, released December 1 of the same year.

As her first picture for United Artists, Mary made *Pollyanna*. It was released January 21, 1920. It was not a story that Mary particularly liked, as she found it too sentimental, and the title character that she played, "the Glad Girl," irritated her.

"I decided," she wrote, "that saintly little creature was just too good to be true."

The story, from Eleanor H. Parker's best-selling novel, is about a crippled orphan who spreads joy and happiness all around her, hence "the Glad Girl." Much to her chagrin, it became the role that is most often identified with Mary Pickford.

8

The Marriage of the Century

By early 1918, Beth Fairbanks had begun to suspect that husband Douglas was having an affair. If this is true, she must have been the last one to hear the gossip. While Douglas kept affirming that he loved his wife, he and Mary had been carrying on a relationship for three years. They might have thought their affair was a secret, but lately they'd been riding around Los Angeles in an open car and were "disguised" in goggles and dusters.

Beth and her son were staying in a New York hotel in April 1918 while Douglas was taking part in the Liberty Loan drives. When he arrived in town and booked a room in another hotel, Beth's suspicions were confirmed.

She went public with her humiliation, informing the press that all the rumours they'd been alluding to were true. She did not, however, mention Mary's name, saying only that the "mystery woman" had a business connection to Douglas. It didn't take Owen Moore long to fill in the blanks for everyone.

Beth Fairbanks filed for divorce on October 22, 1918. At the hearing, two witnesses testified to some of Douglas's other "indiscretions," and Mary's name was kept out of it. The court decided that Douglas Jr. would remain with his mother, which was just as well, because Doug Sr. had never paid much attention to the boy anyway.

In the early part of the twentieth century, society held a dim view of divorce, and because of the stigma attached to it, Mary resisted cutting Owen loose. She was terrified that the bad publicity would ruin her career, that no one would ever want to watch her movies again.

Because the Pickford family's wealth was dependent on Mary's career, Charlotte tried to get Owen to refuse to give Mary a divorce. Like Charlotte, Adolph Zukor, too, was opposed to the divorce. He told Mary she would be letting millions of people down if she went ahead with it. No wonder Mary dithered.

But Fairbanks's patience was wearing thin. He wanted to marry his sweetheart, and he was willing to risk losing his career over it. When Mary asked him, "If the world doesn't approve, will our love be sufficient for our future happiness together?" Douglas assured her that it would. He only wanted Mary for herself.

She described this as "a black and indecisive period" in her life. To make matters worse, Owen had asked for another reconciliation. "I'll even be nice to your mother if you take me back, Mary," he promised. But it was several years too late for that.

In the end, Charlotte suggested that Mary follow her heart, and Owen Moore agreed to a divorce. For a price. He required a settlement of $100,000 dollars. Charlotte herself went to the bank to get him his money.

In February 1920, Mary and her mother travelled to Nevada, where the divorce laws were less strict than those in

California and where she would not have to wait a year before remarrying. Mary Pickford and Owen Moore were divorced on March 2, 1920.

Twenty-six days later, in a small, private ceremony, Mary and Douglas were married at the Los Angeles home of a Baptist pastor. Mary was beautiful in a frothy white dress trimmed with the palest green.

The next day, she returned to work on her current picture, *Suds*, hiding her wedding ring under adhesive tape. In the film, a slapstick comedy, Mary plays another lonely, unattractive Cockney girl. The character, the feisty Amanda, saves a run-down horse named Lavender from the glue factory. She takes him home with her, tying him to a lamp post outside. When it begins to rain, Amanda leads the animal up the outside stairs to her tenement flat.

The horse in the picture was supposed to look half-starved, but it had been staying at the Fairbanks stables and was so well-fed — the animal was now sixty pounds heavier than it had been initially — that Mary and the property boy had to paint ribs on it for the film.

Two days after their wedding, at a small dinner party at their home, Mary and Douglas announced that they were married. The news hit the streets the next day. America's Sweetheart had married everyone's favourite screen hero, and the whole world rejoiced.

When Mary and Doug arrived in New York in June to begin a four-week European honeymoon, the crowd outside the Ritz-Carleton Hotel, where they were staying, went wild with joy. Their hotel suite was packed with reporters, and a delighted Fairbanks suggested they all follow him up to the rooftop, where he performed a handstand on the edge of the roof.

Each evening when the newlyweds attended the theatre, the audience rose to its feet and applauded.

They set sail for Europe on the S.S. *Lapland*, with their personal staff and forty pieces of luggage, leaving Charlotte behind in New York. Mary was hoping to be able to stay in some quaint country inns while they toured Britain. Instead, as the ship docked at Southhampton and roses showered down on them from airplanes, they were mobbed. Everyone wanted to see the world's most famous newlyweds. The pair even looked as if they belonged together: Mary diminutive, fair-haired, and dignified; Douglas dark-complexioned and extroverted, a role model for the healthy, all-American male.

The traffic around their London hotel was snarled for miles, and Douglas had to carry Mary through the crowd in order to get inside. He relished the adulation, but it left Mary unnerved and feeling a little ill.

Night and day, thousands waited for them in the street outside their hotel. On one occasion, while they were being driven through London in an open Rolls-Royce, someone reached out to take Mary's hand and didn't let go, pulling her half out of the car. Douglas had to grab onto her ankles to save her, yelling for their driver to stop.

"When we got out of the car," Mary later wrote, "the crowds closed in like quicksand." They'd gone out for afternoon tea on the Isle of Wight, a place they had expected to find some seclusion. But, as Mary wrote, "... Douglas and I were soon aware that a frantic and uninhibited souvenir hunt was on. When we took inventory later in the day, Douglas had lost all the buttons off his coat and vest, and I had surrendered my handbag, powder case, and handkerchief. Even the hairpins in my curls were gone."

They tried to escape to Holland, but word leaked out that they were coming, and they were met by throngs of screaming fans. The frenzy was repeated in France, where Mary, terrified, was nearly trampled by the mob in an outdoor market on the Left Bank.

When they reached Switzerland and Italy, there were huge, cheering crowds, but fortunately the scene there was less violent. In Venice, when the couple attempted a moonlight gondola ride, a second gondola filled with photographers went along with them.

Mary Pickford and Douglas Fairbanks were Hollywood royalty, the first members of a brand new craze called "celebrity." Only the movies could have attracted such a huge following. Actors on the stage would never have been seen by enough people for this level of popularity to be possible. And the tabloids tried to keep up with the public's insatiable appetite for pictures and gossip.

Silent movies were unique in that they had no barriers of language. "We of the silent screen enjoyed a unique privilege," Mary wrote. "Through our voiceless images we were citizens of every country of the world."

For a year prior to the wedding, Douglas had been living in a large eighteen-acre estate on Summit Drive in Beverly Hills. Once a rustic hunting lodge, it had been completely remodelled, and now Douglas presented it as a wedding present to his bride. The twenty-two room mansion, with a view of Benedict Canyon and the distant Pacific Ocean, came complete with servants' quarters, stables, tennis courts, kennels, fountains, and an oyster-shaped swimming pool. Theirs was the first home in Los Angeles to have a swimming pool set into a formal garden, and in this case, it even had its own beach.

Once they'd settled in, Mary and Douglas put out the welcome mat. Everyone, including the press, who named the place "Pickfair," was made to feel at home. The couple was willing to share their personal lives with their fans and didn't consider the idea of invasion of privacy at this early stage. Before long, the papers began to carry stories about "a day in the life" of the famous couple, and Pickfair became the centre of Hollywood society.

After a day at work, Mary, Douglas, and Charlie Chaplin would get together at Pickfair and show each other their daily rushes, sharing their honest opinions of one another's work. If Chaplin wanted to stay the night, there was even a room in the house reserved for him, although he lived only a block away. Charlotte had her own home below the mountain.

Every evening the table in the dining room at Pickfair was set for fifteen; Douglas loved to invite people home. But he also loved to play practical jokes on them, such as providing them with rubber forks, or wiring a guest's chair so that he received an electric shock when he sat down.

Mary was always ready to play hostess to Doug's eclectic assortment of friends, which included prize fighters, cowboys, and stock car racers rubbing shoulders with lords and ladies, and famous personalities like Helen Keller, Sir Arthur Conan Doyle, or Albert Einstein. Mary herself had few close personal friends, with the exception of Frances Marion, Lillian Gish, and journalist Adela Rogers St. Johns.

After dinner their guests would be invited to join Mary and Douglas to watch movies on a screen that was built into one wall of the living room. If some people considered life at Pickfair a little boring, it was because the residents felt they owed it to their fans to live sober, respectable lives.

No alcohol was served at Pickfair parties. Douglas didn't touch it, and besides, prohibition came into effect in the U.S. in January 1920, although anyone with money had no trouble getting it. At times, the party guests would hightail it to another house where they knew there was a good supply.

Mary continued to be thrifty, a habit left over from her impoverished childhood. But now her closets were filled with furs and gowns from Paris, all the "nice things" she never had growing up. "I never went anywhere," she wrote, recalling her early days. "Never bought clothes, no jewellery."

Mary had grown very fond of Lottie's daughter, Gwynne. When Lottie was divorced in 1920, the child was adopted by her grandmother, Charlotte, and Mary played an important role in raising the little girl.

From left to right: Douglas Fairbanks, Mary Pickford, Charlotte, Jack, Gwynne, and Lottie Pickford, circa 1925.

Following *Suds*, Mary's next picture was a departure from her usual comedies. In *The Love Light*, released January 9, 1921, Mary's character, Angela, tends a lighthouse in an Italian fishing village. One day she discovers a sailor washed up on the rocks below the lighthouse. She takes care of him, and this relationship inevitably develops into a love affair. By the time she discovers that her lover is a German spy, she's pregnant. Angela turns the man in, but before he is captured, he kills himself on the rocks from which he'd earlier been rescued.

The movie was a bold experiment for Mary and not the kind of film her fans wanted from her. Frances Marion made her directorial debut with this picture, and her husband, Fred Thomson, played the part of the spy, obviously as a favour to Frances. It was the only time Mary was ever directed by a woman.

In an effort to help her brother Jack out of a deep depression, following his wife's tragic death, Mary had him co-direct her next two pictures, titled *Through the Back Door* and *Little Lord Fauntleroy* respectively.

Jack Pickford's wife, actress and former member of the Ziegfeld Follies, Olive Thomas, had died an agonizing death after accidentally ingesting bi-chloride of mercury tablets while the couple was in Paris. Whether she had been drinking and had mistaken the tablets for sleeping pills is unknown, but her death was long and painful. Jack was inconsolable.

Douglas Fairbanks was ready to take his own movies in a new direction. He turned from his usual light comedies to making a series of swashbuckling adventures that would forever change his image. The first of these pictures was *The Mark of Zorro*, which came from a magazine story that had been submitted for his approval. The film was released in November 1920.

When Douglas grew a moustache for his role as D'Artagnan in his next adventure film — a favourite childhood story of his, *The Three Musketeers* — it became a trademark that he kept for the rest of his life.

In the picture *Through the Back Door*, Mary plays a Belgian refugee maid, and there is one particularly memorable scene where she ties scrub brushes to her feet and skates across soapy water to clean the kitchen floor. This film was released May 17, 1921, and it served to restore Mary's "Little Mary" image.

With the coming of feature films, the nickelodeons were slowly disappearing, and movie theatres were becoming grand, ornate palaces. Uniformed ushers showed movie-goers to their seats, which were no longer only rickety chairs. Movie premieres were in their heyday in the Twenties, and often the theatre lobby itself would be decorated to reflect the period of the film.

In keeping with this trend of bigger and better, the movies themselves had to get longer and more artistic. Mary had been turning out films of five reels in length, but her next work, *Little Lord Fauntleroy*, was ten.

She played dual roles in this picture, which was set in 1885 and based on the novel by Frances Hodgson Burnett. Mary played the boy Cedric, as well as his widowed mother, Dearest. Audiences were amazed at the double exposure technique that enabled cameraman Charles Rosher to show Cedric (Mary) planting a kiss on his mother's (also Mary) cheek. The scene, which took fifteen hours to shoot, lasted only three seconds on the screen. The picture was co-directed by Alfred E. Green and Jack Pickford, although apparently Jack only showed up when he felt like it.

The film, released September 11, 1921, was one of the biggest hits of that year, grossing more than $1 million. Some critics recognized "the Fairbanks influence" in the way Cedric, Mary's boy character, swaggers when he walks and tosses off handstands with ease.

Mary and Douglas often worked side-by-side on their films, visiting each other's sets and taking their breaks together. Their work day done, they'd often be seen walking off, hand-in-hand.

The couple kept separate production companies within United Artists, and in 1922 they purchased an old studio on Santa Monica Boulevard in Hollywood, renaming the facility the Pickford-Fairbanks Studio. Mary had a fully-staffed bungalow built, and Douglas had a gym, pool, and steam bath added to his office. Douglas, who performed all his own stunts in his films, kept his athletic body in shape by strenuous calisthenics, boxing, running, and fencing. They each had their own trailers, fully equipped as studios, for shooting on location.

Mary's sets were happy places to work, and it was equally pleasant to work on one of Douglas's pictures. Everyone referred to the Pickford-Fairbanks Studio as "Doug and Mary's." The couple was relaxed and happy and very much in love. Beth Fairbanks, too, was happy, after marrying again in 1920. Charlotte still continued to sit in one of the director's chairs on Mary's set, next to the real director.

People remember Mary as extremely kind, a warm and considerate woman, who was always looking out for her people. She always made it a point to thank her extras in person. "No one ever worked for me," Mary said. "We worked together." And no one's suggestion was ever left unconsidered.

One day in 1922, she noticed a little girl who seemed to be waiting for someone in the street across from the studio. When

Mary asked the child why she was there, she learned that the girl's mother had found a job in the studio's wardrobe department. Mary knew there had to be a better arrangement for the girl than having her hang around all day with no one to look out for her. With the mother's permission, she and Douglas gave the child a bit part in one of Douglas's pictures.

The roles of women in society began to change after they won the right to vote in the U.S. in 1920. Movies, too, were becoming more erotic, the female stars shown smoking, drinking, and engaging in risqué behaviour. The popular actress Clara Bow, who fairly exuded sex, was dubbed the "It" girl.

At the opposite end of the spectrum were the characters portrayed by Mary Pickford, Charlie Chaplin, and Douglas Fairbanks. Those innocent, happy, humourous characters with their wholesome values continued to be very popular with movie fans of the day.

On October 1, 1921, Mary and Douglas again sailed to Europe, taking little Gwynne and Doug's brother, Robert Fairbanks, with them. It was another exhausting tour of several countries, and this time it was all done in less than two months. Mary collapsed in London, but she was on her feet again in three days. When they arrived back in New York, she told her fans she would soon be working on a remake of *Tess of the Storm Country*, the film which had been her first success, back in 1914.

The role in the film of the spunky girl on the verge of becoming an adult was Mary's favourite, and now she welcomed the opportunity to bring the picture up to date.

The new version took three times longer to make than the first, because Mary was determined that it would be the best it could be. She had a whole village built for the set. In the end, the picture went $400,000 over budget, but it grossed more than twice what it had cost.

It was released November 12, 1922, and it did so well at the box office that Mary decided the time had come to test the water with some more grownup roles. She began to look around for something to fill the bill.

It was Robert Fairbanks who convinced his brother Douglas to make *Robin Hood*. Always keen to learn a new sport, Doug took up archery in order to play the part, and he soon became expert at it. The full title of the film, released in October 1922, was *Douglas Fairbanks in Robin Hood*, and it was the biggest picture ever made in Hollywood to that date. The authentic sets for the picture became a major Hollywood tourist attraction. Douglas was able to show off his acrobatic skill in the film, plunging down tapestries and leaping about the battlements of a twelfth century Norman castle.

United Artists founders at the Chaplin studios, 1919. From left to right: Douglas Fairbanks, D. W. Griffith, Mary Pickford, and Charlie Chaplin.

The demand for longer, ten and twelve reel films became a problem for United Artists. Mary and Douglas were able to keep up with their quota, and both *Robin Hood* and *Little Lord Fauntleroy* were hugely successful, but Charlie Chaplin was a very slow creator. Of the films D.W. Griffith contributed, only one was a financial success. In the end, he would leave the company, joining Famous Players-Lasky in 1924.

In 1922, starved for product, United Artists formed Allied Producers and Distributors to distribute the films of other artists whose work matched the high standard of the original partners. On behalf of United Artists, Douglas Fairbanks, who loved to travel, set up company offices in several foreign capitals.

Near the end of 1921, a German film called *Passion* opened in New York, and the American public became aware that other countries were producing movies. Mary Pickford, who along with Douglas Fairbanks was among the first to recognize the importance of foreign films, arranged for the director of *Passion*, Ernst Lubitsch, to come to America. She signed him to a contract to do three pictures with her.

Feeling she had taken her little girl characters as far as she could, Mary was now determined to play a real adult role. She had spent $250,000 preparing the script of *Dorothy Vernon of Haddon Hall*, and she intended for Lubitsch to direct her in it.

But when the famed director arrived in America, in October 1922, he refused to do the picture, saying there were too many queens in it. The film was a historical costume drama set in Elizabethan England at the time of Queen Elizabeth I and Mary, Queen of Scots.

Lubitsch's choice was Goethe's *Faust*, which Mary agreed to, until Charlotte, the guardian of her daughter's image, vehemently objected. In the story, Mary's character has an illegitimate baby and then kills the infant. Personally, Mary thought it was one way to get rid of her little girl image once and for all. But saner heads prevailed.

Mary and Lubitsch eventually came up with *Rosita*, a more suitable, but still sophisticated, film. It tells the story of a Spanish king who is in love with a flirtatious little street singer, played by Mary. The story is set in old Seville, with sets so stunning that it was one of the most beautiful of all silent pictures.

Lubitsch had trouble accepting Mary as the final authority on all aspects of the film, and there were frequent disagreements between them. Unlike Marshall Neilan, Lubitsch was used to being the star of his own pictures. One day the man had such a temper tantrum over Mary's refusal to give him the last word that he tore all the buttons off his shirt. His English was so fractured that it caused much hilarity on the set.

Despite this, the picture was finished, and Mary was still convinced that the man was the greatest director in the world. He had been signed to direct her in two more films, but for some reason about which Mary always remained silent, his contract was terminated.

Here finally was a film where Mary played a different kind of role, but she was not pleased with it. She called *Rosita* the worst picture she'd ever made, and she refused to allow the original print or negative to be preserved.

Mary explained, "Lubitsch's reputation had been built on sophisticated comedies ... on the risqué side ... I tried to make *Rosita* very correct, but a little naughty too. The result was disastrous."

Mary was capable of playing a sensuous woman, but she was not "all about sex," the way Lubitsch was.

"I didn't like myself in *Rosita*," she said. "I think it was my fault, not Lubitsch's. We just didn't seem to get together, but I was very proud of the fact that I was able to bring him to this country with no bad effects." Lubitsch went on to sign with Warner Bros. and eventually went to Paramount.

Rosita premiered September 3, 1923, at New York's Lyric Theatre. The critics raved about it, declaring, "no one should worry about Mary growing up." The picture did well in the larger cities, but less so in the small towns in the U.S., where fans may not have been ready for this new image of Mary Pickford.

She announced that her next film, the one she'd hope to do with Lubitsch, would be *Dorothy Vernon of Haddon Hall*, with Marshall Neilan back in the director's chair. Her romantic interest in the film was played by actor Allan Forrest, Lottie Pickford's second husband.

Lottie, who had a small role in the film herself, appeared to have settled down, at least for the time being. Earlier, both she and Jack Pickford had been involved in a major Prohibition scandal. Now, Jack had married another girl from the Zeigfeld Follies, Marilyn Miller, a party girl with a bad reputation. Initially, Mary had serious doubts about the relationship, but when the engagement became official, she tried to accept the girl and even gave the couple a wedding at Pickfair.

Mary's film, *Dorothy Vernon of Haddon Hall*, was released March 15, 1924. Douglas's picture, *The Thief of Baghdad*, a film with a budget of $2 million, opened that same spring.

If it hadn't been for the fact that Fairbanks's teenaged son, Douglas Jr., had recently gained national attention in his first picture, *Stephen Steps Out*, no one would have believed

Douglas Sr.'s age. Now past forty, he was still a fine physical specimen.

Douglas Jr. visited Pickfair occasionally, and he and Mary became good friends. His father however, seemed to resent the young man, most likely because he was a reminder that Douglas Sr. was no longer young.

For the premiere of Fairbanks's film, *The Thief of Baghdad*, the Liberty Theatre in New York had been transformed into a scene from *The Arabian Nights*. People had been gathering outside the theatre for hours, awaiting the arrival of the Fairbanks's limousine.

When Mary stepped out onto the sidewalk, she was nearly crushed by a crowd of 5,000 people. Ever gallant, Douglas hoisted her up onto his shoulders and carried her inside. It had become part of the ritual of their arrival at all their public appearances.

9

Success and Sorrow

After a visit to Toronto in March 1924, where they were guests of the King Edward Hotel, Mary Pickford and Douglas Fairbanks set off one month later on board the *Olympic* for another European tour. The White Star Line had taken great pains to prevent the usual pandemonium among the star worshippers, and they had the passengers board the ship two hours prior to the scheduled departure. No visitors were allowed.

The throng of fans who showed up dockside were too late to see Mary and Douglas embark and had to be satisfied with the kisses the couple threw them from the railing of the ship as it set out to sea.

The trip was another opportunity for Douglas to hobnob with the aristocrats, guaranteeing reciprocal visits to Pickfair. He and Mary were presented to the Kings and Queens of Spain and Norway. Doug's pretensions often amused Mary. A title attached to one's name meant little to her; she liked people for what, not whom, they were.

Reviews for Mary's last picture, the ten-reel costume piece *Dorothy Vernon of Haddon Hall*, which had cost $1 million to make, had been merely lukewarm. Mary considered its poor returns, and those of *Rosita*, her punishment for wanting to grow up on the screen.

"I knew something for certain now," she later wrote. "The public just refused to accept me in any role older than this gawky, fighting age of adolescent girlhood."

Her most loyal fans were women and children, family audiences looking for a return to innocence in the free and easy climate of the Roaring Twenties.

At one point during the filming of *Dorothy Vernon of Haddon Hall*, Mary had to stay calm in the face of certain disaster when the horse she was riding spooked. It happened while shooting a scene on location in Golden Gate Park in San Francisco, where 10,000 spectators had gathered.

Wearing a multi-skirted heavy Elizabethan costume, Mary was riding sidesaddle on the white horse. The camera crew was filming her from a car, driving slowly alongside. Among those in the car was her director, Marshall Neilan. Because Mary had been afraid the horse, "Pearl," might slip on the asphalt of the road, the animal was wearing four special rubber shoes.

Suddenly, for no reason that was apparent to Mary, the horse began to speed up. Mary heard the men in the car shouting at her, trying to warn her that Pearl had lost one of her shoes.

The horse must have sensed that something was wrong, or perhaps it was the close proximity of the car, but it broke into a run, throwing out its front feet, ears back, head lowered. Faster and faster Pearl raced, trying to outdistance the car, while the heavy skirts of Mary's costume flapped wildly against its flank. Straight ahead was the intersecting highway, with a steady stream of cars and trucks moving quickly in either direction.

Praying for a miracle, Mary pulled herself forward, trying to get close to the animal's ears. She stroked the horse's neck, and aware that its former owners had been women and that the horse would be familiar with a female voice, Mary began talking to it. "That's all right now, Pearl." She kept talking, caressing the horse, and trying to calm it.

Just as they reached the intersection, she gave one quick jerk on the reins with both hands. Pearl reared, half stumbled, and landed in a culvert on all four feet, with Mary still in the saddle.

"Automobiles had started putting on the brakes," Mary wrote, "and you can imagine their amazement as Dorothy Vernon of Haddon Hall came tearing out of nowhere, long blond hair streaming in the wind, garbed in an elaborate Elizabethan robe. Poor Pearl was drenched in perspiration and so terrified that the veins and muscles were standing out like whipcords all over her body. I've never seen five more frightened human beings than the men in that camera car."

At the same time as feature-length films came into being and nickelodeons disappeared, magazines about the movies were developing. *Motion Picture Story Magazine* began its life in February 1911 as an in-house publication of the Vitagraph Studio in New York. It caught on quickly and started appearing on the newsstands. Three years later, the publication shortened its name to *Motion Picture Magazine*.

The first issue of Chicago-based *Photoplay Magazine* appeared in August 1911, and it soon moved to the front of the pack. Initially, the focus of these magazines, designed as promotion tools for the films, had been the plots and characters in the movies. But as time passed, and the public wanted to know more about the private lives of the celebrities, the mandate of the magazines changed.

Mary was photographed for the movie magazines looking demure and angelic, back-lit so that her hair was given a halo-like appearance. Her face was everywhere — on postcards, purse-size mirrors, trading cards, buttons, and broaches.

For several years, colour paintings of Mary appeared on twenty-eight inch long panels that were used to advertise Pompeian Beauty Products. "Mary Pickford the world's most famous woman has again honoured Pompeian by posing exclusively for this 1918 panel."

In 1925, in an interview conducted by *Photoplay*, Mary Pickford asked her fans what role they would like her to play next.

"Every now and then, as the years went by and I continued to play (the same) roles," Mary wrote in her memoir, "it would worry me that I was becoming a personality instead of an actress."

Twenty thousand replies to Mary's question came in to *Photoplay*, and overwhelmingly the requests were for her to portray more children and young teens. Some titles suggested were *Cinderella*, which she had already done in 1914 with Owen Moore, *Anne of Green Gables*, *Heidi*, and *Alice in Wonderland*.

Through *Photoplay* Mary sent a thank-you letter to her fans and went on to write the scenario for *Little Annie Rooney*, although she gave the credit for it to her Irish grandmother, Catherine Hennessey. It was to be Mary's last little girl role. She was thirty-three.

The film tells the story of Annie, a twelve-year-old tomboy, who sets out to avenge the death of her father, a New York City policeman. The news of his death reaches Annie on his birthday while she waits for him to come home.

Mary had no trouble turning on the tears when her character realizes her father will never eat the birthday cake she's made him, with its assorted stumps of candles. Nor will he ever wear the striped tie she has knit for him. Mary identified with Annie's grief.

"I imagined what my life would be like without him," she later wrote. "… I really was that bereaved little orphan."

Pathos aside, *Little Annie Rooney*, released October 18, 1925, was a rollicking, mostly funny picture, and it was Mary's first real success in three years. It restored Mary Pickford to the top of the popularity polls.

During the filming of *Little Annie Rooney*, the Los Angeles police department learned of a plot to kidnap Mary and demand a ransom for her release. The informant was one of the plotters.

Their plan was to kidnap several prominent people, including child actor Jackie Coogan and the sultry actress Pola Negri, who had followed Ernst Lubitsch to America and with whom Charlie Chaplin had had a much-publicized affair in 1922–23.

Mary Pickford was to be the first victim. She was to be grabbed on her way to or from the studio after the kidnappers had first overpowered her chauffeur. She was to be gagged, blindfolded, and held captive in a hideout somewhere in Santa Monica until a ransom of $100,000 was paid.

The police were powerless to make any arrests until the would-be kidnappers made a move. They were monitoring the activities of the plotters from a stakeout in a hotel room right next door. The police instructed Mary to carry on with her regular routine.

Every morning, her Rolls-Royce left Pickfair with someone posing as Mary sitting in the back. At the studio, Mary was protected by a plainclothesman. Everyone else thought the man was an extra with the cast until the day he climbed up to sit on a high stool, and his coat opened to reveal a .38 revolver.

Douglas had bought Mary a pearl-handled Colt .45 and taught her how to use it. Every evening Mary and Douglas would leave the studio together, picking up a police escort in another car a safe distance away.

After the plotters were spotted purchasing a gun, and it was discovered that they had rented a house where they planned to hold the victims, the police closed in. There had been no kidnapping. But the experience left Mary badly shaken and a much more cautious woman. Afterwards, Douglas and Mary hired a watchman for Pickfair, installed an alarm system, and acquired some well-trained watch dogs.

When D.W. Griffith left United Artists in 1924, lured away by generous offers from Zukor's Famous Players-Lasky, his replacement as a partner in the company was Joseph Schenck, who also became chairman of the board. Schenck's skills at administration left the founders free to devote more time to doing what they were best at — making movies.

Two years after Schenck joined United Artists, he developed a division called Art Cinema. Art Cinema would go on to finance and produce movies for Norma Talmadge, Rudolph Valentino, Mary Pickford, and Buster Keaton, and distribute movies for billionaire-producer Howard Hughes.

In 1925 Schenck brought the unpopular Sam Goldwyn on board. United Artists needed the money that distributing Goldwyn's films would bring in. When glamour-girl actress

Gloria Swanson decided to become her own producer, she became the latest partner in United Artists.

At the request of the group, Sam Goldwyn developed the United Artists Theatre Circuit, a chain that would distribute United Artists movies. The circuit came to own theatres in Los Angeles, Chicago, and Detroit, as well as the Egyptian and Chinese Theatres in Hollywood, and it had partial interest in the Rialto and Rivoli in New York.

Many stars of the silent films left their signatures and their hand and footprints in wet cement in the forecourt of Hollywood's exotic Chinese Theatre. Mary Pickford and Douglas Fairbanks were the first celebrities to be so immortalized.

In 1926 Mary and Douglas released two of their best films, *Sparrows* and *The Black Pirate*. *Sparrows*, a nine-reel thriller, was Mary's only Gothic melodrama. In it she plays Mollie, the fifteen-year-old guardian of a group of abused orphans, living on a "baby farm" in the swampland of the Deep South. When Mollie attempts to rescue the children from the evil farmer who runs the place, she has to ferry them across a creek that is infested with live alligators. In the film, Mollie makes the treacherous escape with the children while carrying a baby on her back.

When Douglas visited the set and saw just how dangerous the alligators were (all the children in the film were genuinely frightened), he ordered the director, William Beaudine, to use a technique where the reptiles would later be superimposed onto the film. Mary, however, overruled him; she said she'd worked with alligators before.

Sparrows was a lavish production, although less so than Fairbanks's *The Black Pirate*, which was one of the first films to be shot in a two-colour process that was the predecessor of Technicolour. The two films played as a double bill at the Egyptian Theatre in Hollywood.

With both pictures completed, Mary and Douglas once again made plans for an around-the-world trip, which was initially to last two years. On April 3, 1926, Mary, Douglas, and Charlotte sailed from New York aboard the SS *Conte Biancamano*.

Six days later, when they docked at Genoa, Italy, Charlotte was taken off the ship while suffering "stomach trouble." Only when Mary and Douglas had seen her settled in a spa in Florence that was famous for its restorative waters and had been assured that she was in good hands did they resume the tour.

In Berlin the couple attended the European premiere of *Little Annie Rooney* at the Capital Theatre. When Mary and Douglas entered the theatre and the orchestra struck up *The Star-Spangled Banner*, it was the first time an orchestra in Germany had played the American national anthem since the war.

In Russia, where Mary (known to them as "Maruska") was adored, tens of thousands of fans came out to the train station in Moscow to greet the pair. The Russian film industry, still in its infancy, produced *The Kiss of Mary Pickford* in 1927, and footage of Mary and Doug's visit to the country was included in the film.

The couple was in Czechoslovakia when word came that Charlotte was worse. They rushed back to Florence and accompanied Mary's mother back home to the United States.

The Academy of Motion Picture Arts and Sciences was first conceived over dinner at the home of Louis B. Mayer, studio chief at Metro-Goldwyn-Mayer. He and three of his guests — actor Conrad Nagel, director Fred Niblo, and producer Fred Beetson

— began discussing the idea of creating an organization that would benefit the entire film industry.

A week later they invited a number of big names in the business to hear their proposal. Mary Pickford and Douglas Fairbanks became two of the founders of the organization.

The primary goal of the Academy was "to foster technical research and the exchange of artistic and scientific news." Mary liked to refer to it as "the motion picture league of nations."

The Academy was officially announced in May 1927 at a banquet in Los Angeles. Douglas Fairbanks, as the Academy's first president, gave the opening address, and everyone rose when it was time for Mary to come to the podium.

It was announced that there would be an annual presentation of Academy Awards for achievement in the various fields of the industry. From the Academy's earliest days, all its other activities have been overshadowed by the Academy Awards, which would later be called the "Oscars."

The first ever Academy Award for Best Picture was given to *Wings*, a silent film made in 1927 about airmen in the First World War. *Wings* was the first film to show fighter planes in action. Co-starring in the picture were the "It" girl, Clara Bow, and Charles "Buddy" Rogers, a young man who, within ten years, would become Mary Pickford's third husband.

Buddy Rogers was born in Kansas in 1904. He was a musician playing in a jazz band and attending university when, in 1925, his father sent a photo of the good-looking young man to Famous Players-Lasky. The company was looking for new talent, and as a result, Buddy was assigned to the young talent program at Paramount's Astoria Studio in Queen's, New York.

Buddy met Mary Pickford for the first time at United Artists through Hope Loring, someone he'd met at a dance. Loring had written the scenario for *My Best Girl*, the picture Mary was working on at the time. Subsequently, Buddy landed the role of the romantic lead in the film.

The movie, released October 31, 1927, is a boy-meets-girl love story filled with light and warmth, thanks not only to the acting of Mary and Buddy, but also to Charles Rosher's fine camera work.

Mary, playing her familiar role as the sole supporter of a poor family, is a clerk in a five-and-ten-cent store who falls in love with the boss's son, played by Buddy Rogers.

To prepare herself for the role, Mary went to work in a five-and-dime in Los Angeles, wearing her hair pulled back and sporting a pair of horn-rimmed glasses. For a couple of hours and several sales, she went unrecognized.

My Best Girl, was a charming comedy and the picture that made a star out of Buddy Rogers. It was to be Mary's last silent movie.

Mary Pickford had been making $1 million per year ever since 1919, but it had not come without long days spent working. She rose each morning at 5 a.m. and was driven to the studio; often, she was accompanied by her French tutor during these drives so that she could use this time to perfect her French.

Once at the studio, it took three hours to wash and set Mary's hair and to apply her makeup. Filming began at 9 a.m. and could last ten to twelve hours. Later, there were the dailies to view before leaving for home. Dinner was always eaten at Pickfair with Douglas.

Mary also had a number of civic duties to attend to, and Douglas was frequently her good-natured companion at these events. Together they laid cornerstones, cut ribbons, opened fairs, and were the guests of honour at numerous banquets. A Hollywood movie premiere, no matter whose picture it happened to be, did not begin until Mary Pickford and Douglas Fairbanks were in their seats.

Douglas and Mary happy together at Pickfair, circa 1922.

In 1926 Douglas had bought a beach house in Santa Monica to serve as their retreat, and for the first ten years of their marriage the two were almost never separated.

The couple also owned 3,000 acres in San Diego County that was once part of an historic Spanish land grant. They called it Rancho Zorro, after the fictional character Douglas was so fond of. Today, the area is home to a huge development known as Fairbanks Ranch.

Douglas had Mary to thank for the gradual improvement in his relationship with his son, Douglas Fairbanks Jr. He and Mary had taken to calling the young man "Jayar," and for his part, Jayar agreed to call his father "Pete."

The younger Fairbanks had been an actor since 1923, when he appeared in the film *Stephen Steps Out*. But he got his first real break in 1925 with a part in the movie *Stella Dallas*. Over the years, Douglas Jr. deliberately avoided playing the type of swashbuckling roles for which his father was famous. He took to the stage, impressing both Mary and Doug Sr. He also began to publish short stories and articles, often accompanied by his own drawings.

All things considered, life was good for to the world's most public couple. But when it was determined that Charlotte was suffering from terminal cancer, everything started to fall apart.

Mary blamed herself for an accident that had ostensibly caused a lump in her mother's breast, which eventually killed her. Charlotte had been rummaging in a trunk, looking for some costume material for Mary during the filming of *Little Annie Rooney*, when suddenly the lid of the trunk fell down, striking her on the breast. She didn't tell Mary about the incident until they were on the ship four months later, returning to the States from the aborted world tour. But Charlotte knew something was very wrong. Later, as her condition worsened, Charlotte refused to have surgery, trying various less invasive methods instead.

Mary took a year off work, a first for her, and she and Douglas moved into Charlotte's beach house to look after her. Unfortunately, neither Charlotte nor Mary was able to talk to each other about the seriousness of Charlotte's illness. They both pretended not to know the truth, and Mary compensated for her fear by being overly cheerful. She did her crying alone in the bathroom.

"From the day I learned the truth about Mother's condition," Mary later wrote, "I spent three long years in a hell that only a demon could conceive."

When Charlotte died, March 21, 1928, her eldest daughter went into hysterics. She lashed out like a wild animal at anyone who came close to her, very nearly falling through a plate glass window. Even Douglas couldn't restrain her, and he received a fist in the face for trying. When Mary finally came out of it, she was puzzled by the expression on the faces of the people around her and the whiteness of Douglas's lips.

The thing that brought Mary back to her senses that day was, typically, her concern for someone else. One of Aunt Lizzie's daughters, Mary's cousin Verna, who was eight months pregnant, was sobbing uncontrollably. (Lizzie and her family had earlier moved from Toronto to California.) Mary immediately took it upon herself to comfort the young woman, putting her arms around her and reminding her of her condition: "You know my mother wouldn't want you to risk losing your baby, Verna dear."

Charlotte's death was a devastating blow for Mary. The two had been so close that it was as if each one had completed the other. How was she ever going to be able to live without her?

Unable to seek solace in the Catholic Church, because of her divorce and remarriage, Mary turned to Christian Science, and gradually she began to put the pieces of her shattered life back together.

Exactly three months later, on June 21, 1928, Mary Pickford did what had been unthinkable while Charlotte was alive. She walked into a New York City beauty parlour and asked to have her long hair cut off. It was a historic moment.

"Are you sure that you're not going to regret this, Miss Pickford?" The nervous hairdresser lifted the mass of hair that fell down Mary's back to well past her waist.

"I'm quite sure," Mary replied. Now that she was in the chair, in front of the mirror, she had to go through with it. Besides, the press photographers were there to take pictures.

For a moment, as he picked up the scissors, Mary thought the man was going to faint. She closed her eyes. Before she knew it, it was over.

Photographs taken at the time show Mary's new hairstyle, a cap of naturally wavy, golden hair, just touching the back of her neck and curling gently against her cheeks. Now Mary was ready to play a new type of role. A girl with sex appeal. A girl with "It."

Richmond Hill Public Library
Renew Item Receipt

User name: LU, SHOW YUAN
(MS)
Item ID: 32971012145615
Title: Mary Pickford :
Canada's silent siren,
America's
Date due: November 27,
2014 11:59 PM

www.rhpl.richmondhill.on.ca

10

The Trouble with Talkies

With the arrival of commercial radio broadcasts in 1920, it was only a matter of time before movies with sound would make their debut.

In 1926 Warner Bros. produced *Don Juan*, starring John Barrymore. It was the first feature-length film to use the Vitaphone, a sound-on-disc device that provided sound effects and music for the film, although not yet dialogue. The soundtrack was printed on a record, rather than on the film itself, and it played while the film was being projected on the screen.

The following October, the almost bankrupt Warner Bros. released *The Jazz Singer*, the movie that effectively signalled the end of the era of silent films.

By making use of the Vitaphone, the movie included some scenes with synchronized dialogue, as well as six songs performed by actor Al Jolson. For the most part, the audience was enthusiastic, although some were of the opinion that talking motion pictures were just a passing fad, and there were others who hoped that's exactly what they would be.

Mary Pickford, for one, was nervous about the idea of abandoning the universal language of pantomime, and she hoped the whole thing would blow over. Making movies with sound was going to cost the studios millions. Everything would have to move indoors. It meant building stages with sound-proof walls and hiding microphones from the camera.

The actors would have to learn not to lower their heads when speaking, otherwise the microphones would not pick up their voices, and the noisy cameras would have to be contained in large soundproof booths, taking up valuable space where the front lighting used to be. Theatres, too, would need to be wired for sound.

The sound technician became the most important person on the set, with more control than even the director, who found himself no longer able to shout orders to the actors. Neither would there be any musicians providing music to get the actors in the mood for the scene. It was "quiet on the set!" and tourists were no long welcome in the studio.

The fear now was that the everyone's favourite actor would not have the type of voice the movie goers had imagined that he had. Segments of recorded dialogue were quickly inserted into silent movies that had already been filmed so that they could be billed as "talkies."

The voices of the stars of United Artists were first heard on March 29, 1928, in a radio show that aired in select theatres. For the broadcast, which was hosted by the president of the Dodge Motor Company, Douglas Fairbanks introduced Mary Pickford, Charlie Chaplin, D.W. Griffith, Gloria Swanson, Norma Talmadge (company head Joseph Schenck's wife), and two newcomers to

United Artists, Dolores Del Rio and John Barrymore (the brother of Lionel). Each actor spoke for a few minutes on a subject of his own choosing.

Mary and Douglas had never been worried about how the actual sound of their voices would be received, because they'd been well-tested on the stage. Mary had rather a small voice, but she'd learned how to project it, and Douglas's baritone matched the roles of the dashing hero he usually played.

Unlike those actors with a stage background, stars of the silent films had another concern: they had never had to learn lines before. Mary was one actor who *had* always learned the lines for the roles she played in her silent movies, even though they would never be heard.

United Artist's Norma Talmadge was one of a number of Hollywood actors whose careers came to an end with the introduction of talkies. Talmadge had been a glamourous star of silent movies, but when it was discovered that she talked with a flat Brooklyn accent, which even speech lessons did little to improve, she retired from the business.

Actor John Gilbert, known as a great lover on the silent screen, had his career ruined when the sound man gave his voice too much treble and he came out sounding like a woman.

Mary started searching for a film to launch herself into the new era of talking pictures. She liked what she saw on Broadway in 1928, where Helen Hayes was starring in the play *Coquette*.

Lillian Gish urged Mary to buy the screen rights to the play, and it went into production, with Sam Taylor directing, at the end of the year. In the film, Mary plays the character Norma Bessant, a wealthy young flirt from the South.

At this time, Mary's personal life was in shambles. She was close to a nervous breakdown and was still grieving the loss of her mother. In the midst of filming, Mary fell apart emotionally and wept for twenty-four hours straight, shutting down production. Then she fired her cameraman, Charles Rosher, because he stopped filming when he saw a shadow fall on her face. She said later that firing her longtime cameraman had broken her heart. Everyone was feeling the strain of making a sound production.

But Mary had to keep challenging herself. She was getting strong competition now from actresses like Clara Bow and Greta Garbo.

Mary in Coquette, *her first talkie, 1929.*

Coquette, released April 12, 1929, was the first talkie to be made by a major star of the silents. Although 3,000 theatres in the States were unable to show it because they had not yet installed new sound equipment, it made more money than any of Mary's previous films. She won the Academy Award for Best Actress for *Coquette* in 1930, the first Academy Award given to an actress in a talkie.

On the day of Mary's history-making haircut, in June 1928, she had left Douglas back at their New York City hotel while she visited the beauty parlour. When she returned and stood in front of him to remove her hat, revealing her new jazz-age crop, Douglas Fairbanks fell into a chair, moaning, his eyes welling with tears.

"But I told you I was going to do it," Mary protested.

"I know, honey," Douglas said, "but I didn't think you meant it. I never dreamt you'd do it."

Mary had expected that type of reaction from him. But she had been unprepared for the negative response she got from the public. They acted as if she'd betrayed them, and they sent her letters filled with insults.

"You would have thought I'd murdered someone," she later wrote, "and perhaps I had, but only to give her successor a chance to live." Hurt, Mary became defensive, suggesting that if her curls were the only thing about her career that mattered, she might as well retire.

But she had other concerns as well. She had been noticing a change in Douglas. "There was a time," Mary wrote in her memoir, "he realized youth was slipping from him. At that point a strange fever and restlessness settled upon him, and possibly a growing loss of confidence."

Douglas had been warned by his doctors that he should be taking it a little easier now, rather than continuing to tax his muscle-bound body the way he had for years. But he had ignored the advice and continued his regular regime of strenuous exercise.

Early in 1929, he played his favourite role: D'Artagnan in *The Iron Mask*, a silent movie with a talking prologue. Afterwards, he and Mary decided to make *The Taming of the Shrew* together, a first for them. It would be the first sound production of a Shakespearean play, and they decided it might provide a needed kick-start to their careers.

The play was adapted for the screen by Sam Taylor, who was also the director. Right from the start, Mary sensed a lack of interest on Doug's part.

He took his time coming to the studio each day and didn't seem to care that he'd kept everyone waiting — he did his morning exercises and took his sunbath, arriving on the set at noon for a 9 o'clock call. When he did appear, he frequently did not know his lines and had to read them from large blackboards set up beyond camera range. He took long breaks and wasted time, playing his usual practical jokes on the set. Mary was on edge the whole while, wondering what his next move would be.

As she described it, "The strain and tension of those months was a tragic change from the atmosphere of friendly teamwork that had prevailed in the Pickford-Fairbanks Studio for so many years. Everywhere in Hollywood our studio had come to be regarded as the happiest 'lot' of all."

Unlike Douglas, Mary had trouble speaking in Shakespearian verse. She hired a voice coach to help her add some grandeur to her small voice, although the director disapproved. He wanted the old Pickford antics, contrary to Mary's vision for the film.

Mary described the making of the movie as her finish. "My confidence was completely shattered, and I was never again at ease before a camera or a microphone." In the film, she appears most comfortable when her role calls for her to be silent.

With Douglas's slapstick comedy, energetic leaping about, impressive speaking voice, and with Mary's usual mischievousness, it was a version of Shakespeare's play never seen before.

Still, the critics seemed to approve. Released October 26, 1929, the film opened to good reviews. The *New York Times* named it one of the ten best pictures of the year. The fact that it didn't do well at the box office could be blamed on its being released just after the crash of the stock market.

At the same time as the sound version of *The Taming of the Shrew* was released, there was also a silent version made for those theatres not yet equipped to show talkies. Like many others in the industry, United Artists wasn't sure movies with sound were not just a fad.

The cost to the studios of converting to sound, coupled with the effects of the Great Depression, meant that smaller, independent companies just couldn't compete. When the dust settled, there remained eight studios. The big five were MGM, Paramount, Warner Bros., Fox, and RKO, which was a newcomer in 1929, and the three smaller studios were Columbia, Universal, and United Artists.

With *The Taming of the Shrew* finished, another world tour seemed to be in order for Douglas and Mary. This time, they would visit Gwynne at school in Lausanne, Switzerland. Gwynne had been about thirteen when Charlotte died, and ever since, when she wasn't away at school, she had lived at Pickfair with Mary and Douglas.

To satisfy Douglas's wanderlust, the pair continued on from Switzerland to Greece, Egypt, China, and then Tokyo, Japan, where Mary was once again nearly crushed by her fans. From there, it was Hawaii and then home. They'd been away four months.

As always, Douglas revelled in the crowds of adoring fans, diving right into their midst and willingly trying out all the native dishes he was served. It was all a bit too much for Mary, and at times she begged off, preferring to stay quietly in their hotel room. The world's most celebrated marriage was starting to look a little shaky.

For Douglas, the trip had been just what he needed. In fact, it had been such a success that he and Mary wrote a book about it. They titled it *Our Trip Around the World*, but the book was never published.

Mary got busy planning a remake of *Secrets*, a silent picture from 1924 that had starred Norma Talmadge. Mary's version, a talkie, would be titled *Forever Yours*.

The news that Douglas was considering retirement may not have come as a surprise to Mary. His finances had been badly affected by the crash of the stock market, and now he had taken up the game of golf and become obsessed with it.

It was Doug's theory that once a man was on the downhill slope, the sooner he got to the bottom, the better. With that pronouncement, he took off for Scotland and the Walker Cup Golf Tournament. It was the first time he'd ever left Mary behind.

Marshall Neilan, whose work with Mary had been so brilliant in the past, was hired to direct her in *Forever Yours*. But everything seemed to go wrong. Neilan had lost his edge. He'd run into trouble lately with some of the producers due to his worsening problem with alcohol, and he had been directing only short slapstick pictures.

There was also a problem with the script of the play, and when Mary saw the first rushes, she was unhappy with the picture, finally deciding that it didn't have enough action in it.

Kenneth MacKenna, the leading man, had been a poor choice to play opposite Mary, because he was so much younger. She and Neilan argued frequently about Neilan's heavy drinking during the filming. Halfway through production, Mary shut it down, cut her losses (which were considerable), and went off to Europe to be with Douglas.

She let herself be talked into her next picture, a sex farce titled *Kiki*. It had been the head of United Artists, Joe Schenck's, idea. Through his Art Cinema division, he would produce and finance the film, and Mary signed a contract with him for a flat fee, working as an actress for another producer for the first time since she had left Adolph Zukor.

Mary had always taken her preparation for a picture seriously, but talkies made her anxious, and this time, besides taking dancing lessons, she hired someone to coach her in developing a French accent for her role as the sexy French chorus girl.

Released March 14, 1931, *Kiki* opened at the Rialto Theatre in New York. It was the first Mary Pickford film ever to lose money for United Artists. Mary called it the worst picture of her career, except for *Rosita*. It bombed at the box office. Had Mary not already known that box office sales had been in a downward spiral ever since the novelty of sound movies had worn off, she might have assumed that her fans did not approve of her playing such a sensuous role.

Douglas Fairbanks tried one more film, *Reaching for the Moon*, but in it he appeared lost, a man past his prime, and it seemed doomed to failure. On the night of its New York premiere, early in 1931, he boarded a ship headed for the Far East. His next two pictures were travelogues, based on his journeys to all corners of the globe. They garnered little attention.

Perhaps Mary could sympathize with her husband's fear; she, too, was feeling uneasy. They were both getting older, and the years aren't kind to actors whose fans refuse to let them age gracefully on the screen. As Mary approached her fortieth birthday, she felt her popularity slipping away.

She had always liked to travel but now said she liked being at Pickfair better. She loved it when the whole family gathered around the pool on the grounds. Robert Fairbanks, his wife, and their four daughters would come, and Gwynne would be there during the summer and on holidays. Jayar and his wife, actress Joan Crawford, whom he had married in 1929, when he was only nineteen, would join them occasionally.

Jayar and his father had gotten closer in recent years, especially after the death in 1927 of John Fairbanks, Douglas Sr.'s eldest brother and a man who had been like a father to him.

Jack Pickford, Mary's younger brother, was in the American hospital in Neuilly, near Paris, suffering from "progressive multiple neuritis," likely a result of years of alcohol abuse. Early in the new year, 1933, Mary got word that Jack was dying. She immediately sent a wire to say she was on her way, but he died the next day, January 3, 1933, before she could get to his bedside. He was only thirty-six.

The best way for Mary to cope with another loss was to get to work on her next picture. She decided to take a second look at *Secrets*, the picture she had shut down while it was in production as *Forever Yours*.

British actor Leslie Howard was signed to co-star with Mary in *Secrets*, and Frank Borzage was the director. Released March

15, 1933, the nine-reel picture is said to be the best of the Pickford talkies, finally giving Mary a firm, dramatic role. Although the picture lost money, it was nothing like the failure *Kiki* had been.

But Mary's audiences were getting smaller. The public had lost interest in many of the silent film stars, and Mary was among them. She couldn't even count on Douglas for support in this difficult time; he was in Europe again. She was bewildered by his constant need to travel and his desire to play golf all over the globe.

Douglas Jr. was of the opinion that his father didn't like making talkies and that he had lost interest in the movie business. But had he also lost interest in Mary and life at Pickfair?

Mary never knew what Douglas's plans were, or when he was coming home, and all she got from him were excuses. His secretary, a man who travelled with him, said that while Doug was away, he never stayed in the same place longer than one night. Douglas was a man in motion, and Mary couldn't keep up with him.

11

The End of the Fairy Tale

Douglas Fairbanks and Mary Pickford had gone to Europe together early in 1931, when Mary's picture *Kiki* was finished. Mary had had to return to the States at Easter, and Douglas had stayed behind to play in a golf tournament.

At a party in London that spring, he had met and fallen in love with a tall, willowy former chorus girl with an impressive name: Lady Sylvia Ashley. Twenty years younger than Douglas, Sylvia was separated from her husband, Anthony Ashley-Cooper, the eldest son of the Earl of Shaftesbury.

Douglas and Sylvia began to be seen together in all the hot spots around town, and the London rumour mills were soon abuzz. The news of the affair inevitably reached Mary back in Los Angeles. She didn't share the news with anyone, keeping it to herself for some time.

Mary justifies her silence in her memoir, *Sunshine and Shadow*: "One of the great penalties those of us who live our lives in full view of the public must pay is the loss of that most cherished birthright of man's privacy. Receiving so much from the public, we sacrifice our right to this privilege accorded to others. But we are as human as the next fellow. Sorrow, embarrassment, and humiliation are our heritage too. So we cannot be blamed, in time of crises, for expecting the refuge of a little privacy."

Mary kept herself busy; she was having renovations done at Pickfair. The 1932 Olympic Games were coming to Los Angeles, and so, too, was Douglas.

When he did come home, Fairbanks finished making *Mr. Robinson Crusoe*, another picture based on his travels. It was a talkie released in August 1932. As expected, Douglas stayed on for the games. And then he was gone again.

In 1933, after completing *Secrets*, Mary sailed to Europe to meet her husband for a skiing holiday in St. Moritz. This may have been the point at which she confronted him about his affair. She was home again, by herself, within six weeks. Perhaps she was able to take some comfort in the good reviews that were coming in for *Secrets*.

Douglas didn't seem to be able to make up his mind about what he wanted. Although he kept assuring Mary that Sylvia meant nothing to him, he was unable to stay away from her for any length of time.

Finally, he sent Mary a cablegram, announcing that he intended to stay in England. Mary could remain in Pickfair, if that's really what she wanted. There was some suggestion that he was hoping Mary would decide to join him on the other side of the Atlantic and take up the lifestyle of international traveller that he had espoused.

Mary was desperate to get him to come home and thought that maybe she could provide him with the little nudge he needed.

One day over lunch with a close friend, she shared the contents of Douglas's cablegram with her companion. Also lunching with them that day was Louella Parsons, gossip columnist for the Hearst newspaper chain. The friend persuaded Mary to let Louella read the message. Mary agreed, but begged Louella not to print anything that would hurt Doug. After all, she wasn't planning to take any action yet, thinking Douglas would eventually "snap out of it."

"I've got to be patient with him," she explained. "There's nothing I want to say to him for the present except that I love him."

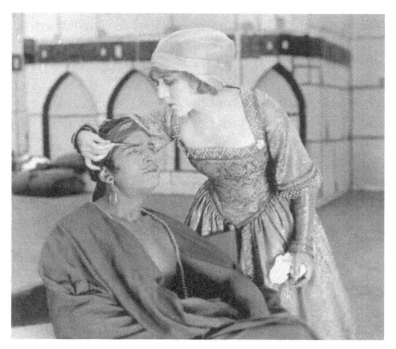

Mary and Douglas in costume together. Pickford is dressed as Dorothy Vernon of Haddon Hall *(1924) and Fairbanks as* The Thief of Bagdad *(1924).*

Never one to risk being scooped on a story of this magnitude, Louella Parsons went straight to work. On July 3, 1933, the headlines of the *New York Daily News* proclaimed, "Doug and Mary Part."

Mary was devastated. Douglas would be furious; neither one of them needed this kind of publicity. Everything she'd wanted left out of the story had been printed. "Where there had been only heartbreak and hope," she wrote later, "a full size scandal now stared me in the face."

As she had feared, hordes of reporters and photographers gathered outside the gates at Pickfair, clamouring for an interview with her. She sent word to them through her press agent. "Yes, we're having a separation. But there are no plans for divorce."

In London Douglas Fairbanks said, "No comment."

His brother, Robert, called the whole thing "a tempest in a teapot."

Weeks went by with no further word from Douglas. Someone had to make the first move. On December 8, 1933, Mary petitioned for divorce. Immediately afterwards, she travelled to New York City to spend the Christmas holidays with nineteen-year-old Gwynne. Together, they planned to see some plays on Broadway and to go ice-skating in Central Park.

Douglas remained in Europe. It was the first Christmas they'd spent apart since their marriage.

For one week, beginning December 22, Mary appeared in a stage show in New York City. Her part was a short comedy, a playlet, called *The Church Mouse*, which preceded the show's main attraction. Because Mary was hoping to make a return to Broadway, the playlet was a good place to start.

The production of *The Church Mouse* was a huge success, and on the last day of Mary's appearance, the police had to be called in to control the crowd. Then followed a two-month tour of the play in the Paramount theatres on the east coast.

There had been a plan in 1933 for Mary to appear as Alice, the only live character in a Walt Disney adaption of Lewis Carroll's *Alice in Wonderland*. All the other characters in the film would be animations.

Cartoons were already very popular, taking over where silent movies had left off. Long an admirer of the young Walt Disney, Mary had urged United Artists to bring him on board, and Disney had signed a distribution contract with the company in 1931. It had provided the financial boost that the struggling United Artists needed.

Mary did a Technicolour screen test for her Alice project, but there was a lot of hesitation on Disney's end. He seemed less enthusiastic about the project than Mary was, and when she heard that Paramount was making an all-star version of the story, she bowed out.

Douglas Fairbanks was no longer able to hide his infidelity from the press when, in April 1934, he was named as co-respondent in Lord Ashley-Cooper's divorce. Knowing how humiliated Douglas would be, having his name attached to the scandal, Mary sent him her sympathies.

In the summer of 1934, Mary and *The Church Mouse* arrived, triumphant, in Toronto. Among those on hand to meet her at Union Station when she got off the train was her old doctor and friend, Dr. G. B. Smith. Mary stayed at the Royal York Hotel, and the hometown crowds followed her everywhere. She and Dr. Smith rode together in an open car through the streets of downtown Toronto with ticker tape raining down on them.

At City Hall, Mary was greeted by throngs of fans and well-wishers. Happy to oblige the press, she got on a bicycle and rode it to her birthplace, telling the crowd, "I love all of you, my fellow Torontonians." It seemed as if no one in Canada had heard the news about the end of the marriage of Hollywood's Royal Couple.

Back in England, Douglas was finishing *The Private Life of Don Juan*. It would be his last picture. The film was produced by London-based Alexander Korda, whose productions would now be distributed in America by United Artists, thanks to an arrangement made by Fairbanks. A year later, Korda would become a partner in United Artists.

Mary found plenty to occupy her mind. She was doing some writing, looking at scripts for her hoped-for Broadway comeback, and thinking she'd like to make another movie. She wrote a self-help booklet titled *Why Not Try God?* It was a combination of Christian Science teaching and her own plucky optimism. With Christian Science, she'd found a religion in which she was comfortable.

The following year, 1935, she wrote another book, titled *My Rendezvous with Life*. One imagines that Mary found strength in gathering her thoughts for the creation of these inspirational booklets.

Several screen actors were presenting radio shows at this time, and the Mary Pickford Stock Radio Company, her own radio theatre, began to broadcast a series of shortened versions of Broadway plays. The show made its debut on the air in the fall of 1934, with *The Church Mouse* as the first in the series.

Microphones still caused Mary some anxiety, however, and the critics were less than enthusiastic about her performance. In 1936 she tried another radio show, *Parties at Pickfair*, featuring Mary Pickford and her celebrity friends in informal chats over dinner. It aired every Tuesday evening on the Columbia

Broadcasting System (CBS). After thirteen weeks, it, too, went off the air.

With her niece Gwynne taking a very small role, Mary starred in the stage version of her movie *Coquette* in May 1935 in Seattle. She toyed with the idea of taking it on tour but didn't. She'd written a novel called *The Demi Widow* and now discussed with its ghost writer, Bette Burns Gromer, the idea of turning it into a play. Then she changed her mind.

Mary was struggling. She seemed restless and lost, taking on new projects, trying to find something that would make her happy. Her friends were worried about her. Of particular concern was the fact that Mary was drinking. It was the old family sickness. When it had started for Mary is hard to pinpoint, but it had become worse following Charlotte's death. Then there was the realization that talkies had made her movies obsolete. And now there was the indecision over Douglas.

Douglas Fairbanks made repeated attempts at a reconciliation with Mary, and for a while it looked as if it might happen. He would arrive at Pickfair and take Mary out for long drives. They went to the Santa Monica beach house together; they dined by candlelight. People who saw them together remarked on how happy they looked.

Douglas spent some time in seclusion at his Rancho Zorro, thinking things over, but inevitably he would sail back to Europe alone. He had changed, and as Mary wrote, "Something had gone. It was as though his spirit had fled."

Doug and Mary's friends couldn't believe what was happening. The couple loved each other, but the situation now seemed to be beyond their control. Powerless to stop it, they let themselves be swept along to its sad conclusion. The divorce became final January 10, 1936.

Although Mary was now no longer his wife, Douglas came back to Los Angeles, where he showed up at Pickfair every day, trying to woo her back; he bought her a diamond bracelet, which she refused to accept, and he suggested that they retire together to a place like Switzerland.

Douglas had even enlisted the help of his ex-wife, Beth, happily married since 1920 to musical comedy star Jack Whiting, to try to win Mary back. It didn't work.

It took almost a year for Douglas to accept the truth. Even as he set out for New York and the ship that would eventually take him back to Europe, he was sending messages to Mary, pleading with her. She refused to budge.

His son, Douglas Jr., who was with him in New York, where they planned to spend some time together, arrived at the hotel one morning and discovered that his father had unexpectedly checked out. He'd sailed the night before. A telegram had been delivered to Doug's room after he'd left. It was from Mary. She was ready to forgive him; he should come home.

But it was too late. On March 7, 1936, Douglas married Lady Sylvia Ashley.

Much later, when Douglas and Sylvia were ensconced in the Santa Monica beach house, which he'd gotten in addition to the ranch in the divorce settlement, Douglas would occasionally drive up to Pickfair. He and Mary would just sit together quietly and talk. They both knew what a terrible mistake they had made. And according to Mary's niece Gwynne, Mary was never the same after the divorce.

Then came the loss of another member of Mary's family. Lottie Pickford died suddenly of a heart attack on December 9, 1936. She was forty-one. She had lived all her life in the shadow of her more famous sister, and their relationship had been strained for years. Mary admitted that her fondest memories of "Chuckie" were of those brief years when they were little girls together, playing in the snowy streets of Toronto.

The old rivalry between the sisters, begun as youngsters vying for their father's favour, had persisted into their adult lives. Mary had seldom provided Lottie with the same opportunities to further her career that she'd given her baby brother, Jack. Lottie had made just eight feature movies in her lifetime, while Jack had made forty.

Mary had been able to overlook Jack's many indiscretions, but had never been very forgiving of Lottie's. Knowing that, her guilt must have made her grief more acute.

Lottie and Jack Pickford had been close all through their lives. When Jack had died four years earlier, Mary was said to have remarked that the better part of Lottie had died with him.

Charles "Buddy" Rogers had been Mary's co-star in her last silent picture, the 1927 romantic comedy *My Best Girl*. He was a pleasant young man, and everyone liked him. As an actor, he was mediocre, but he could have been better if the studio had wanted to work with him. Instead, they kept giving him second-rate pictures, telling him the good roles would turn up. He just needed to be patient.

In 1931 Buddy asked Paramount (formerly Famous Players-Lasky) to release him from his contract. He wanted to spend more time with his music, the thing that gave him the greatest satisfaction. He could play several instruments well, and he dreamed of conducting. With financial help from Mary, he formed a dance band called "The California Cavaliers," the first of a number of bands that Buddy Rogers would lead.

Buddy Rogers had been in love with Mary Pickford ever since she'd played opposite him in *My Best Girl*. Mary had pretended not to notice. But during the years of turmoil with Douglas, he was always there for her. Once in a while, they'd even managed to get away together.

After the divorce, Mary dated other men, while Buddy was touring with his band. She tried to put on a happy face for her young suitor. It was obvious to everyone that Buddy, eleven years her junior, adored her. He asked her to marry him, but she kept him waiting several months for an answer.

Compared to Douglas, Buddy had a lot going for him. He was young, very good-looking, loved Mary, and was as loyal as a puppy dog. She knew he would never break her heart. Even the Fairbanks family was fond of him.

Mary began to dream of a quiet life, maybe a small house and time to go horseback riding and play tennis. Maybe a life with Buddy. After her last two pictures had been financial failures, she had told a reporter that she would never make another movie, and she had no ambition now to go back on the stage.

Buddy came to spend the Christmas of 1936 at Pickfair. He and Mary were married the following summer, on June 24, 1937.

The small outdoor wedding was at the home of Hope Loring, the author of the scenario for *My Best Girl*. When Mary and Buddy knelt on satin pillows to say their wedding vows — from which Mary had removed the words "to obey" — the bride looked much younger than her forty-four years.

Among the thirty wedding guests were Gwynne, Mary's cousin Verna, and Lottie's fourth husband, John Lock, now a widower. Mary had banned newsreel photographers from the wedding, and there was only a small group of still photographers.

For the lavish reception back at Pickfair, with a guest list of 300, Buddy refused to allow any press pictures to be taken.

The newlyweds embarked on a honeymoon cruise to Hawaii accompanied by Gwynne and four other friends. Five thousand fans met them as their ship docked in the harbour at Honolulu. To Mary the cheering crowd reminded her of the old days. But Buddy was too shy to leave the ship.

12

Life After Douglas

The administration of United Artists was in a constant state of flux. Joe Schenck and Sam Goldwyn, between them releasing forty-four pictures from 1928–38, were the only ones bringing in any money for the company. Douglas Fairbanks had persuaded Alex Korda to come on board, but that was followed by Schenck resigning as president. His Art Cinema had folded in 1933 after suffering serious financial loses, including those incurred from Mary's picture *Kiki*. Al Lichtman replaced Schenck in 1935. When he resigned after only three months, Mary took over. It was during her time as president that the company lost its distribution contract with Walt Disney. A year later, United Artists elected A.H. Gianinni to replace her.

D.W. Griffith, who had returned to the company from Famous Players-Lasky in 1927 — not as a partner this time, but with Schenck's Art Cinema — had lost his creative touch, and his contract with United Artists had ended in 1933. Actress

Gloria Swanson, too, had left, after being forced to sell back her stock.

Now that their days of starring in movies were over, Mary Pickford and Douglas Fairbanks functioned only as producers and stockholders in United Artists.

In an effort to provide the company with some much-needed product, Mary had joined Jesse Lasky, one of Paramount's original founders who was at the time with Fox, to form Pickford-Lasky Productions. They planned to produce four pictures in the first year. *One Rainy Afternoon*, the first film, released in 1936, was not very successful. It was followed by *The Gay Desperado*. Both pictures starred English-American actress Ida Lupino, and although the second movie did a little better than the first, it was not enough to keep Pickford-Lasky Productions from folding in 1937.

Upset that everyone else at United Artists was earning money from the distribution of his pictures, but contributing nothing themselves, the ever-disgruntled Sam Goldwyn tried to gain control. He wanted to see the company under new management, calling the rest of the members "parasites," and insisting, in 1939, that he was the only one with the right to vote. He felt he should be able to elect his own board of directors.

The relationship between the principals went from bad to worse. Goldwyn wanted out of his contract, but United Artists needed his films. They battled in the courts for two years, costing everyone dearly.

Mary had tried living in Buddy's Los Angeles home when they were first married, but it wasn't long before she persuaded him to move with her back into Pickfair, where all her memories were waiting.

A selfless husband, Buddy supported and encouraged his wife to continue the pursuit of her many interests. One of Mary's projects in 1938 was to write a series of newspaper articles, in the form of interviews with celebrities, for the *New York Journal.* That same year, she and Buddy launched a new company, Mary Pickford Cosmetics Inc., with Mary herself appearing in the advertisements.

"... every preparation had to measure up to her fastidious standards. Moreover, Miss Pickford insisted on keeping the prices low, so that all women might use and enjoy these beauty aids."

The line of cosmetics included face creams, soap, lipstick, dry rouge, and powder, and was touted as "Beauty on a Budget." Trial-sized samples of the creams were sold for ten cents each, or three for a quarter. Unfortunately, the venture was short-lived.

Douglas Fairbanks and Sylvia had come back to Los Angeles in September 1939, just before war broke out in Europe, and they were living in the beach house in Santa Monica. In spite of his doctor's advice, Douglas had continued to maintain his rigorous exercise regime.

One day in December, he felt what he thought was indigestion — a pain in his arms and chest. His brother, Robert, insisted on calling a heart specialist, who determined that Doug had suffered a mild heart attack. The doctor prescribed several weeks, possibly months, of bedrest.

Robert and Jayar had both spent some time with him during that day, December 11. Earlier, Douglas had told Robert that, in the event of his death, he would like Robert to deliver a message to Mary. It was their old secret code, "by the clock," a reminder that he would always love her.

Jayar had sat reading to his father before saying goodnight to him for what would be the last time. Around midnight Douglas's nurse heard a noise from the bedroom, where Douglas was alone with his dog, and upon entering the room, discovered that Fairbanks had died.

Mary was in Chicago at the time, travelling with Buddy and his band. At four in the morning on December 12, 1939, Mary's niece Gwynne called her with the news. She had only to hear the tone of Gwynne's voice to realize what had happened. "Don't tell me," she said, "my darling is gone."

Out of respect for Buddy, Mary held back her tears until she was on the train alone, returning to New York. She'd phoned Douglas's old friend, Charlie Chaplin, to give him the sad news, but he'd already heard it from Jayar.

Although Mary and Chaplin had been estranged for years, their shared grief provided them an opportunity to talk about days gone by. They reminisced by telephone for over an hour, remembering the happy times together at Pickfair, how they used to watch each other's films, and recalling Doug's hearty laughter at Chaplin's antics on the screen.

Mary, who had, back in 1916, written, "No one else has ever had or could have had such a smile as Douglas Fairbanks," now prepared a statement for the press.

"I am sure it will prove a consolation to us all to recall the joy and the glorious spirit of adventure he gave the world. He has passed from our mortal life quickly and spontaneously as he did everything in life, but it is impossible to believe that vibrant and gay spirit could ever perish."

Neither she nor Charlie Chaplin could bring themselves to attend the funeral.

* * *

Mary had always had a special rapport with children, and it grieved her that she'd never had any of her own. Every child she ever worked with in her films brought out Mary's maternal instincts. Douglas Fairbanks Jr. remembered how, when he was six, his father had brought Mary to meet him for the first time. She had gotten right down on the floor with him, asking if she, too, could play with the child's toy train.

In 1943, while Buddy was a flying instructor in the Navy Air Corps and Mary was embroiled in the increasing wrangles at United Artists, the couple adopted a six-year-old boy from an orphanage. They named him Ronald Charles Rogers. Less than a year later, another adopted child, a five-month-old baby girl, Roxanne, joined the family.

While they were still youngsters, the two children brought Mary and Buddy much happiness, and the couple gave Ronnie and Roxanne all the things a child could wish for. Unfortunately, as children of celebrities, they often saw more of their nannies than of their parents.

When he wasn't playing golf or polo or touring with his band, Buddy Rogers was still working occasionally on stage and in films. In 1950 he would host a television program called *Cavalcade of Bands*.

Mary liked to join Buddy on the road whenever she could, but she was also busy at least twice a week, entertaining at Pickfair, conducting house tours, and giving parties there for military men and women who were visiting Hollywood.

In 1943, as part of her work on behalf of the Canadian war effort, Mary helped develop plans to build a house in Toronto that would be the first prize in a raffle to raise funds for several

Mary and Buddy Rogers and their adopted children, Ronald and Roxanne, circa 1946.

war charities. The bungalow-style house, built at 90 Glenwood Crescent in East York, was valued at $15,000, with tickets selling for a dollar apiece.

Mary financed the construction from the sale of her old family home in Toronto, and she came to the city to attend the opening of the Mary Pickford Bungalow on May 26, 1943.

In the summer of 1949, Mary invited forty blind veterans from the Sawtelle Veterans' Hospital in Los Angeles to a garden party at her home. Actress and singer Dinah Shore, who was a favourite of the troops during the Second World War, came up to Pickfair to sing for the guests. It was so successful that the outing became an annual event.

David O. Selznick, head of Selznick International Pictures, had been distributing his films through United Artists since 1935, and in 1941 he'd joined Mary and Charlie Chaplin as a full partner. United Artists had bought Sam Goldwyn's shares back, and he left the company that same year for RKO Radio Pictures, who would distribute his films almost to the end of his career.

Then, in 1943, Alex Korda left. Although nothing seemed to bother Charlie, Mary was worried about the situation. So worried, in fact, that when Jayar had asked about the possibility of producing his pictures through United Artists, Mary had advised him to avoid the company.

United Artists had advanced Selznick money when he first came on as a partner, but when the man took three years to release his next picture for them, Charlie Chaplin brought a lawsuit against him. Mary tried to reason with him, but Chaplin accused her of siding with Selznick. Had Charlie forgotten, Mary wondered, just how long she and Douglas had waited for *his* first picture?

Selznick left in 1947, and Mary began to think the time had come to put the company up for sale. But Charlie wasn't answering his phone.

The board of directors suggested instead that Joe Schenck come back to help find a new president, re-organize the company, and try to mend relations between the two remaining partners, Mary and Chaplin. Again, Charlie Chaplin resisted.

In 1947 Mary, Buddy, and Ralph Cohn formed Comet Productions and co-produced *Sleep My Love*, starring Claudette Colbert, Robert Cummings, and Don Ameche. The picture turned out to be Mary's first financial success in years.

As part of her release agreement with United Artists, Mary decided to hold the premiere of the picture in Ottawa on January 13, 1948. The event would be a benefit for the United Nations Emergency Save the Children Organization (UNESCO). Among the special guests for the occasion were Canada's prime minister, William Lyon Mackenzie King, and the governor general, Viscount Harold Alexander.

A huge crowd of Mary's fans turned out to welcome her to Ottawa. After walking in high heels through the snowy streets from the station, Mary attended a Rotary luncheon at the Chateau Laurier. The rest of her day was spent giving back-to-back interviews. Mary was tired but, as always, gracious and obliging.

Following only a brief rest in her hotel, she went to dinner with the prime minister. There was alcohol served with the meal, and Mary had a little too much to drink. By the time she arrived at the premiere, held at the Elgin Theatre, she was a little unsteady on her feet.

A National Film Board sequence shows her arriving at the theatre by car with the prime minister. Both are wearing fur coats, Mary in white fox. She blows endless kisses to the crowd and curtsies when she is introduced to Governor General Alexander and his wife.

It was not like Mary to let her guard down in public. For years Buddy Rogers had tried to hide his wife's drinking. Or, if it was suspected, to make light of it. "Oh, that little *dickens*," he'd remark lovingly. "Once she starts, you know, she just can't seem to stop."

In 1949, Mary, Buddy, and a friend named Malcolm Boyd opened a radio and television production company. They called it Pickford-Rogers-Boyd (P.R.B), and set up company offices in New York City, where Mary also rented temporary living accommodations. Boyd was a young man who had left his job in advertising to start a business that put actors on the air to promote their movies.

Over the years, by renting out the eight-acre lot that was the Pickford-Fairbanks Studio in Los Angeles, United Artists had had a steady source of income. Joseph Schenck had used the lot for his Art Cinema productions. It was also the place where Douglas and Mary made their best films in the 1920s, and it was filled with happy memories for Mary.

Sam Goldwyn had received one-fifth of the shares in the lot when he became a partner in United Artists back in 1925, and he, too, had used the studio for his pictures. All the while, he was snapping up more shares whenever they became available. When Douglas Fairbanks died, Goldwyn talked Doug's widow, Sylvia, into selling him those shares as well. By 1949 Goldwyn owned thirty-nine shares; Mary owned forty-one.

United Artists was in grave financial trouble in 1949. Its new president, Gradwell Sears, sent Mary and Charlie Chaplin a letter warning them of the situation. Two years later, after she and Lester Cowan had co-produced a flop, *Love Happy*, a picture that featured the Marx Brothers and did nothing to ease the company's difficulties, Mary persuaded Chaplin to let lawyers Arthur Krim and Robert Benjamin take control of United Artists as trustees of its stock. Both men were already familiar with the movie business.

The lawyers raised half a million dollars immediately and set out to find product for the company. They were able to buy some low-cost movies from another bankrupt company and acquired the pictures *High Noon* and *The African Queen*, which proved to be fortuitous for United Artists. By 1952, the company was out of debt, and lawyers Krim and Benjamin became half-owners.

While admitting that she and Charlie Chaplin had had their differences over the years, Mary wrote in her memoirs that if people knew something about Chaplin's miserable childhood, they would be more understanding of his unique personality.

In 1889 Charles Spencer Chaplin had been born in London to parents who were music hall entertainers. The couple separated when Charlie was three. He and his half-brother, Sydney, who later served as Charlie's business manager, lived off and on with one parent or the other. The father was an alcoholic, and their mother became mentally unstable, eventually having to be institutionalized.

Charlie was sent to a workhouse for a time and then to a school for paupers. His father died when the boy was twelve. Charlie joined a troupe of young male dancers and landed a small role in the play *Sherlock Holmes* in 1903.

After touring the U.S. with Fred Karno of Karno's London Comedians in 1910 and 1912, Charlie decided to make America his home. He first worked at Keystone Studio, where he appeared in short comedies for Mack Sennett, playing his first role as the little tramp "Charlie," wearing baggy pants, a bowler hat, huge shoes, and swinging his walking stick.

In the early days, after Chaplin had gone over to Mutual Studios, his spectacular salary had caused Mary Pickford to demand similar rates for herself from Famous Players. No "pie-throwing comedian," as she referred to him, was going to be paid more than she was.

The first time Mary ever saw Charlie Chaplin was in a Los Angeles restaurant in 1912, where she was dining with Charlotte. Mary said she thought the slight, dark-haired man with the delicate hands looked like a violinist rather than a comedian. Later, she would praise his wildly successful film persona, the Tramp, saying Chaplin "put a mustache on the mask of comedy."

Mary put up with Chaplin because of their mutual affection for Douglas Fairbanks, but in truth they couldn't stand each other. He criticized her business sense, and she railed against the length of time it took him to make a picture.

One explanation given for this was the fact that Charlie Chaplin never filmed from a completed script. Because the man was a perfectionist, he did retake after retake as the story slowly unfolded. Only when he was satisfied with what he'd done so far did he move on toward an ending.

Mary and Chaplin had battled over United Artists so much that it had affected the company's stability. In the end, without Douglas to tease them into getting along, they just avoided each other. But Mary was a trooper, and she kept these hostilities out of the public's eye.

Chaplin was criticized for never becoming an American citizen, and although he had raised funds for the war effort during the First World War, he didn't support that of the Second World War. This raised the public's ire. Comparatively, although she always kept her Canadian citizenship, Mary was an American by marriage. When the maple leaf was adopted 1965 to replace Canada's Union flag, Mary asked the Canadian embassy in Los Angeles for a flag and promptly had it run up the flagpole at Pickfair.

Chaplin and Mary held widely opposing political views, with Charlie's far to the left of Mary's ultra-conservatism. But when Charlie was branded by the press as a communist sympathizer, it was Mary who stood up for him. No one, she said, should be condemned on mere hearsay.

Chaplin had taken his family to London in 1952 for the premiere of his long-awaited movie, *Limelight.* It would be his last picture for United Artists. When his re-entry visa was revoked, Chaplin decided not to come back to the States, and in 1955 he sold his shares in United Artists. In spite of their quarrels, it broke Mary's heart to see another link to Douglas gone. After the superior court put her old production lot up for auction, she lost a further connection to Douglas Fairbanks when Sam Goldwyn outbid her for it.

As for D.W. Griffith, he had died of a cerebral hemorrhage on Christmas Eve 1948, derelict and alone. With Chaplin's departure, Mary was now the only one left of the original founders. United Artists was doing well, however, and in 1956 Mary sold back her shares for $3 million. Why keep them, she asked, when Douglas and Mr. Griffith were gone?

* * *

One day, back in 1919, Mary had arrived at her Hollywood studio, taken a hammer, and nailed a tin can to the wall. Curious, the others on the set gathered around to read her hand-lettered sign: "Please help others to help themselves by sparing any change you have."

Before long everyone was dropping coins into the can. The idea caught on and spread to all the other studios in Hollywood. People in the industry dug deep into their pockets.

The Motion Picture Relief Fund (MPRF) was officially established in 1921, and Mary, who had kick-started the fund for needy actors with money left over from her work selling Liberty Bonds, served on the board long after her career had ended.

In 1932 Mary was instrumental in introducing the Payroll Pledge Program, a payroll deduction plan for studio workers, who would then give one-half percent of their earnings to the MPRF. She firmly believed the industry must help its own. Her early days spent in poverty were never far from her mind.

After Biograph cameraman Billy Bitzer had a heart attack, Mary saw to it that he was moved to a private hospital, and she made sure that the MPRF paid his bills and gave him a little money to live on.

By 1941 the MPRF had raised enough money to be able to buy the land to begin to build the Motion Picture Country House in Woodland Hills, California. As well as providing a place of residence for deserving performers, a full-scale hospital and a theatre were later added. It is still operating today as the Motion Picture and Television Fund Country House and Hospital. It was here that Marshall Neilan died of throat cancer in 1958.

* * *

"The world's been wonderful to me," Mary said in an interview in 1955. "*People* have been wonderful to me. I like to try to give back."

Throughout the 1950s, she worked tirelessly in support of her many charities. In April of that year, she and Mamie Eisenhower, the wife of the American president, launched a savings bond drive. For seven weeks in twenty-six cities, Mary managed a successful series of speaking engagements, overcoming her usual fear of microphones.

For years Mary tried to atone for a thoughtless, racist remark she'd made about people of the Jewish faith. The guilt she suffered for her insensitivity sickened her, and she did everything she could financially to compensate. She gave generously to help the Jewish cause, including her support for the Mary Pickford Building at Los Angeles' Jewish Home for the Aging. She and Buddy Rogers broke the ground for the new building in 1948. She was also the recipient of three honorary degrees in the humanities in her later years.

Mary's book of memoirs, *Sunshine and Shadow*, was released in 1955 and garnered good reviews. Mary is reported to have said she enjoyed writing the book but resented all the cuts made by the publisher, wishing she could have told the whole truth, "the best and the worst of everything."

When daughter Roxanne was enrolled in a lycée in Spain, Mary and Buddy used to travel to Europe to visit her. Roxanne was living with Mary's niece Gwynne in Barcelona. Later, Roxanne would attend a private school in Switzerland. Divorced in 1944 from her first husband, Gwynne had married Bud Ornstein, an executive with United Artists.

Mary and Buddy's son, Ronnie, had received his education at a prep school in New York State. The teen years had been difficult for the troubled youth. He had turned cold towards Mary, refusing to get along with her. After a teenaged marriage, and by then already the father of two, Ronnie had tried to take his own life. Both Ronnie and Roxanne became alienated from their adoptive parents in later years, although Mary continued to provide for them financially.

At least she had Jayar. He remained a close friend and welcome guest at Pickfair, where he used to bring his children. Mary often lamented the fact that Douglas Sr. never got to meet his three lovely granddaughters.

A highly decorated soldier in the Second World War, in 1948 Sir Douglas Fairbanks Jr. was knighted for his support of many worthy causes, especially for his work with CARE, which sent food to postwar Europe.

The George Eastman House, a film and photographic archive in Rochester, New York, held the first Festival of Film Artists on November 19, 1955. The ceremony included the inaugural presentation of the "George" award, founded to honour those still living who had contributed the most to the silent film decade, 1915–1925.

Five actors, actresses, directors, and cameramen were chosen by more than 300 of their fellow artists. An article in Rochester's *Democrat and Chronicle*, November 20, 1955, reported, "The occasion ... brought to the city 11 personalities in motion pictures who are numbered among the greats of the realm." The veteran producer Jesse L. Lasky presented the awards. Among the winners were actresses Mary Pickford and Lillian Gish, and directors Marshall Neilan and Frank Borzage. Thirty-one-year old Charlton Heston accepted an award on behalf of Cecil B. DeMille. Winners who were absent included Norma Talmadge and cameraman Charles Rosher, both of whom were ill. Gloria

Swanson was in Rome, and Charlie Chaplin, still banned from entering the United States, was living in Europe.

Mary Pickford, as the principal speaker at the event, told funny stories of her fellow actors, and after the showing of clips from old movies containing the best performances of all the prize winners, including Mary's *Little Annie Rooney*, she remarked that perhaps laughter was what was missing from films nowadays.

On Easter morning 1956, Mary invited 200 silent film alumni to Pickfair, including some from her Biograph and features days, as well as some leading ladies who'd played opposite Douglas. It was a garden party on the manicured grounds of Pickfair, and Mary was a gracious hostess. Photographers from *Life* magazine were as welcome to wander through her home as her old friends and colleagues.

For women who in their youth were beautiful, the ravages of time would feel particularly cruel. Mary believed that her audiences expected her to be "Little Mary," young and lovely forever, and since that was impossible, she chose to withdraw.

She might have been better off had she accepted the advice of her friend Lillian Gish and found a way to continue her show business career. Lillian and her sister Dorothy Gish went back to the theatre and continued working on the stage. They both had the ability to play women of any age, and their audiences loved them even as they grew older.

To Mary's credit, knowing old age could not be avoided, she embraced the cause of the elderly, supporting a state bill to house the old and sick. In 1961 she was the Beverly Hills delegate to the first White House Conference on Aging. Initiated by President John F. Kennedy that year, the conference has been held every decade since.

Mary returned to Toronto, for what would be her final visit, in May 1963. She was seventy-one, and Buddy accompanied her. Mary appeared as a mystery guest on the CBC television quiz show *Front Page Challenge.* The format of the show involved the panel being presented with a major news story and then having to identify a hidden personality — someone who was connected to the story. Once she was revealed, Mary and Buddy enjoyed a lively discussion with the panelists.

A major tribute to Mary Pickford, a retrospective of fifty of her films, was presented in Paris in October 1965 by the Cinémathèque Française. Mary attended the month-long event and delivered her address on opening night in perfect French.

She spoke lovingly of the many characters she had played in her films, how they became as real to her as actual people, and how she took them home with her at the end of each day. Wistfully, Mary admitted that she often wished she could meet them in real life. But through her artistry, she had made those characters come to life for the rest of the world.

Mary had been delighted to attend the retrospective in Paris, but afterward she went home and disappeared from public view.

She stayed inside the walls of Pickfair, coming out only to attend the occasional meeting or to go for a car ride with Buddy or Roxanne. She was content, for the most part, to live with her memories of Charlotte and Douglas. Showing signs of chronic heart disease, Mary began to spend a lot of her time in bed. She had fallen and broken her collarbone, and a cataract operation in 1970 left her shaken.

By that time she was seeing no one except for Buddy, Lillian Gish, Frances Marion, her friend Adela Rogers St. Johns, Jayar (whom she often confused with his father), and Gwynne, whose daughter was married at Pickfair in 1970. Once in a while, Mary would agree to speak to a reporter by telephone.

Adela Rogers St. Johns admitted that on her visits the two often talked of Douglas, and Buddy came to the conclusion that his wife sometimes thought she was still married to Douglas Fairbanks.

In May 1971, as part of a worldwide celebration of Mary Pickford's films, the Los Angeles County Museum of Art exhibited ten of her features. Mary would not be attending, but prior to the event, she invited the press to her home. When they arrived, Buddy informed them, with apologies, that Mary couldn't see them. Instead, she sent her love and a taped message.

In Toronto a plaque honouring Mary was unveiled May 27, 1973, on the grounds of the Hospital for Sick Children, at 555 University Avenue, near the site of Mary's birthplace. The ceremony was arranged and sponsored by the Ontario Film Institute.

Mary was not there, but she sent her regrets in a letter, reminding the people of Toronto that she "always remained rooted" in her Canadian childhood. In her absence, Buddy did the unveiling.

That evening, the Ontario Film Institute arranged for a special showing at the Ontario Science Centre of *My Best Girl* from 1927, the only picture in which Mary and Buddy had appeared together. A decade later, a bust of Mary by artist Eino Gira would be unveiled next to the plaque.

By the time Mary won her second Academy Award, in 1976, an Honorary Oscar "in recognition of her unique contribution to the film industry and the development of film as an artistic medium," she was no longer able to walk, having spent so much time in bed.

The award was presented to her at Pickfair, her acceptance video taped and played later at the Academy Award ceremony, where Buddy was shown, silver-haired and weeping, in the audience.

Many people felt it was cruel and exploitive to have aired the tape. The sight of the tiny birdlike woman and the sound of her quavering voice as she accepted her award shattered any illusions that Mary Pickford was somehow still young. How could she be? She was eighty-four years old.

On May 25, 1979, Buddy rushed his wife to Santa Monica Hospital. She had suffered a stroke. Mary lapsed into a coma, and death came to her peacefully on May 29.

13

Legacy

In an interview with *Photoplay* magazine in May 1931, Mary Pickford had let it be known that she intended to add a codicil to her will, one that would ensure that her films were destroyed upon her death.

To this end, she had been buying up all her old negatives, including thirty of the shorts she had made with Biograph. "I would rather be a beautiful illusion in the minds of the people," the article quotes Mary as saying, "than a horrible example on celluloid. I pleased my own generation. That is all that matters."

Mary's old friend, Lillian Gish, appalled at the idea of destroying films, reminded her that her pictures weren't hers to destroy; they belonged to the public. Fortunately, Mary changed her mind. She did, however, keep her films out of public view until 1970, on the grounds that people of later generations would misunderstand them.

Mary had already burned twenty-one prints of *Rosita* and seventeen of *Pollyanna*. It had been common practice for the studios to destroy all their spare prints; space was needed in their vaults. Through United Artists, Mary and Douglas Fairbanks had both sent their spare prints off to the George Eastman House in Rochester, New York, where they were melted down so that the silver could be recovered from the nitrate film.

Eight months before his death in 1939, Douglas Fairbanks Sr. had donated prints of his major films to the film archives of the Museum of Modern Art in New York.

Finally, in 1945, Mary began to give her collected films to the American Film Institute at the Library of Congress in Washington. She stipulated that they were to be used for research and reference only. As mentioned, she did not allow commercial release of her pictures until 1970.

Unfortunately, due to financial cutbacks within the government, the task of transferring the old nitrate negatives and prints onto safety stock, which should have been urgent, was delayed. Only thirteen of Mary's features had been duplicated by the time the funds ran out entirely.

Due to the fact that nitrate film becomes chemically unstable over time, by the time Mary's collection was inventoried a year later, ninety reels had already been lost. Some entire features were beyond saving, including her first three: *The Bishop's Carriage*, *Caprice*, and *Hearts Adrift*.

In 1951 Mary gave the George Eastman House permission to help save her films, and in the next five years, eight productions were transferred onto acetate stock. The process was still too slow, however, to keep up with the decomposition of the originals. In 1956 Mary donated enough money to copy twenty-six features and twenty-five Biograph shorts — all that was left at the Library of Congress that were in good enough shape to save.

The Library of Congress, a public archive, has the Mary Pickford Film Collection in its Motion Picture, Broadcasting and Recorded Sound Division. There is also a theatre named for Mary, on the third floor of the library's Madison Building.

With a grant from the Pickford Foundation, the Academy of Motion Picture Arts and Sciences was able to buy, for its Margaret Herrick Library, a collection of over 3,000 stills from film historian Robert Cushman. These are not the movies themselves, but rather still photographs that were taken from the film to promote it. That collection covered Mary's features from 1915–18, but more were needed.

The library's collection has continued to grow, and today it covers stills from all of Mary Pickford's fifty-two features from 1913–33, as well as most of the Biograph shorts from 1909–12.

The Margaret Herrick Library in Beverly Hills is a non-circulating research facility with the most extensive collection of movie-related materials ever assembled. It boasts a collection of over 100 million photographs. The Mary Pickford Collection includes movie posters, books related to Mary, her correspondence, her famous contracts, papers, movie stills, and portraits. The building that houses the library has been known since 2002 as the Fairbanks Centre for Motion Picture Research, in honour of Douglas Fairbanks Sr.

In 2003 the Mary Pickford Foundation, which had been formed back in 1958 to help those less fortunate and to encourage others to help themselves, opened the Mary Pickford Institute for Film Education in Los Angeles. Its purpose is to teach filmmaking to young people who might not otherwise have the opportunity. For more than fifty years, the Mary Pickford Foundation has provided tens of thousands of individuals and organizations with scholarships and financial assistance.

In 1999 Canada honoured its "Queen of the Silents" posthumously with a star on Canada's Walk of Fame, on King Street in Toronto's theatre district. As well, Mary was one of four "Canadians in Hollywood" pictured in 2006 on a set of postage stamps. The others were Lorne Green, Fay Wray, and John Candy. The set was introduced to collectors at the World Philatelic Exhibition in Washington, D.C., in May 2006. Of all the stamp items offered for sale by the ninety postal authorities from all around the world that were in attendance, this "Canadians in Hollywood" set of stamps was one of the most popular.

Few today can know what Mary Pickford's early films meant to the young generation for which they were made. An American teacher, writer, and critic, the late Edward Wagenknecht, someone who watched the development of silent films during his boyhood years, explained, "It was the sheer wonder of motion that caught and enthralled me, and it is impossible for any youngster today to really understand how marvellous that was."

People who don't know Mary's films well don't appreciate the range and variety of her work. They tend to think she portrayed nothing except sweet little girls or silly romantic heroines. In the opinion of film historian Robert Cushman, who died in 2009, this view "seriously distorts film history." Mary Pickford was "an actress of inexhaustible versatility and dramatic range. She probably did more for the development of acting for the screen than anyone, performer or director, during the whole era of silent pictures."

Mary was so much more than "the girl with the golden curls." She made fifty-two feature-length movies but portrayed a young girl in only seven of them. Her characters were tough and resilient, feisty and independent. And every one of them was different.

Mary made two hundred films in twenty-five years. Aside from being an actor, producer, director, and film executive, she was also a shrewd businesswoman. She was never shy when it came to contract negotiations, and she proved she was ahead of her time by demanding that she be paid the same as her male counterparts. She insisted that her movies be sold separately and not as part of a package with other Famous Players pictures.

As one of the founders of United Artists, Mary ensured that she had total control over her films. She was a founder and life member of the Academy of Motion Picture Arts and Sciences, having recognized the influence the art of motion pictures has on our culture.

Silent film was the only great art that was unique to the twentieth century. And Mary Pickford was there for the full span of its life.

Epilogue

Following a private funeral, Mary Pickford was laid to rest in the family plot at Forest Lawn Cemetery in Los Angeles. At the time of her death, Mary's estate was worth $50 million. The largest part of it was left to the Mary Pickford Foundation in order to continue the support of her charities.

Within the year, Pickfair was put up for sale, selling in 1981 to Jerry Buss, the owner of the Los Angeles Lakers basketball team. The household furnishings and Mary's belongings, except for her papers, scrapbooks, and photographs, were to be sold at auction.

Mary had bequeathed the Star of Bombay, a blue-violet sapphire weighing 182 carats (36 grams), to the Smithsonian Institute in Washington. Originally, the sapphire was a gift to her from Douglas Fairbanks Sr. Today, it is housed in the Smithsonian Institute's Museum of Natural History.

Even before the Pickfair auction began, some of the smaller valuable items disappeared from the house, taken by persons unknown. People were still trying to get a piece of Mary Pickford.

Included in the auction, among the sets of dishes and the silk bedspreads, were some of Mary's vintage costumes, a few that had belonged to Douglas, and also some mementos from their wedding — Mary's tiny wedding dress, her negligees, and Douglas's monogrammed kimono. Even Mary's twelve-inch curls, which she'd kept as souvenirs following the history-making haircut, went on the auction block.

In 1988 Pickfair was sold again, this time to multimillionaire Meshulam Riklis and his movie actress wife, Pia Zadora. Two years later, deciding it was beyond restoration, they had the house torn down and replaced with a modern mansion. Only the gates to Pickfair remain.

Buddy Rogers remarried in 1981 and built a new house on the section of the Pickfair property that had been left to him. He had chosen some of the furniture for his new house from Pickfair and had one room filled with Mary's photographs, portraits, and honours. Buddy died in 1999 at the age of ninety-four.

Mary's first husband, Owen Moore, had been found dead on the kitchen floor of his home in Beverly Hills in June 1939. It was two days before his body was discovered. The actor had never managed to quit drinking for long, although after his divorce from Mary, he had tried many times. He had married silent film actress Kathleen Perry in 1921 and went on to make more movies, the last one being *A Star is Born* in 1937. His death was attributed to cerebral hemorrhage.

Mary and Buddy's adopted daughter, Roxanne, had three marriages, the last ending with her husband's death in 1996. She died April 17, 2001. After 1970 Ronald seems to have slipped out of the public eye altogether, and his whereabouts today are unknown.

Jayar, Douglas Fairbanks Jr., who considered Mary his second mother, had a successful career in films and television and wrote a book of his memoirs, which he titled *Salad Days*. He and actress Joan Crawford had been divorced in 1933, and Douglas Jr.'s second wife, Mary Lee Hartford, with whom he had three daughters, died in 1988. Douglas Jr. died May 7, 2000, in Manhattan. He was ninety.

Charlie Chaplin received an Honorary Award from the Academy of Motion Picture Arts and Sciences in 1972. He came out of exile in order to accept the award and received the longest ovation in Academy Award history, lasting a full twelve minutes.

Because of Chaplin's political difficulties, his 1952 film, *Limelight*, hadn't been shown in Los Angeles. The picture was re-released twenty years later and won the 1973 Academy Award for Chaplin's original musical score.

Charlie and his family did not remain in the States after the ceremony, however. He preferred to live out the rest of his years in Switzerland. He was knighted in 1975. Sir Charles Spencer Chaplin died in 1977, two years before Mary Pickford. In spite of efforts by Jayar, the two were never reconciled.

Chronology of Mary Pickford (1892–1979)

Mary and Her Times

1892

April 8. Birth of Gladys Louise Smith, the future Mary Pickford, at 211 University Ave., Toronto, Ontario, Canada. She is the first child of Charlotte Hennessey and John Charles Smith.

1893

June. Birth of Lottie (Charlotte) Smith, second child of Charlotte and John Smith. The birth is never registered.

1895

Birth of Jack (John) Smith, youngest child of Charlotte and John Smith. The birth is never registered.

Canada and the World

1892

The Kinetescope, a device to record and reproduce objects in motion, is completed. It was commissioned by Thomas Edison and invented by his assistant, William Dickson. The Kinetescope enables a single viewer to see moving pictures.

1893

February 23. Lord Stanley, governor general of Canada, donates the Stanley Cup as a hockey trophy. It is first awarded to the Montreal AAA hockey team.

1895

The Lumière Brothers unveil the Cinématographe in Paris. This invention projects moving images onto a screen some distance away, enabling several

Mary and Her Times	*Canada and the World*
	viewers at a time to see moving pictures.
1898 February 11. Death of John Charles Smith, father of Gladys, Lottie, and Jack. His death, at the age of thirty, is the result of a work-related injury that caused a blood clot in his brain.	**1898** The Edison Company sends a cameraman to Cuba to film scenes of the Spanish-American war.
1900 January 8. Gladys and Lottie Smith make their theatrical debuts in *The Silver King*, a stage play presented at the Princess Theatre in Toronto.	**1900** Canada sends a second contingent of volunteer soldiers to the Boer War in South Africa, where descendents of the Dutch fight for independence from Britain.
November 24. At the close of a second production of *The Silver King*, "Baby Gladys Smith" becomes the Valentine Stock Company's official child actress.	Canadian-born Reginald Fessenden transmits the first wireless broadcast of the human voice over a distance of 1.6 kilometres, from Cobb Island, Maryland.
1901 The Smith family goes on the road with *In Convict Stripes*, beginning a life of barnstorming across the U.S. and Canada that will last for almost six years.	**1901** December 12. Marconi sends the first wireless trans-Atlantic radio signal, from England to St. John's, Newfoundland.
	With the arrival of electricity, lights are strung in New York City from 13th to 46th Streets, creating Broadway's "Great White Way."

Mary and Her Times	**Canada and the World**
1903	**1903**
The Fatal Wedding opens in Pottsville, PA, for a one-night stand. All the Smiths have parts, with Gladys billed as "Baby Gladys."	Silver is discovered at Cobalt, in northern Ontario.
	Canada loses the Alaskan Boundary Dispute to the U.S.
1904	**1904**
Gladys and Lottie tour in *The Child Wife*.	Charles Saunders develops Marquis Wheat at the Dominion Experimental Farm in Ottawa. This hardy strain will bring prosperity to Canada's prairies when it is commercially established in 1911.
1905	**1905**
Gladys plays in *The Gypsy Girl*.	Saskatchewan and Alberta join Canada as the eighth and ninth provinces.
November 5. The whole family appears in the Chauncey Olcott production *Edmund Burke*, opening at Brooklyn's Majestic Theatre. It plays until May 1906.	Cooper-Hewitt mercury-vapour lamps enable filmmaking to move indoors.
	Canadian runner Tom Longboat, an Onondaga from the Six Nations Reserve, wins the Boston Marathon.
	The first filmmaking companies arrive in Los Angeles.
1907	
May 18. When Gladys's road tour of *For a Human Life* ends, she is determined to find another way	

Mary and Her Times	*Canada and the World*

to earn a living for herself and her family.

December 3. Under the direction of David Belasco, Gladys Smith, now Mary Pickford, appears on Broadway in *The Warrens of Virginia*.

1908

May 16. *The Warrens of Virginia* ends its Broadway run, then goes on the road for its second season.

1908

Anne of Green Gables, by Canadian Lucy Maud Montgomery, is published.

1909

January. *Warrens* plays at Toronto's Royal Alexandra Theatre. Critics praise Mary's performance.

March 20. *Warrens* ends its successful touring season at the West End Theatre in Harlem after a total of 190 performances.

April. Mary goes to the American Mutoscope and Biograph Company in New York, looking for work in moving pictures.

April 20. Mary Pickford makes her film debut in *Her First Biscuits*. She will play forty-five roles for director D. W. Griffith in 1909.

1909

To control the film industry, the Motion Picture Patents Company (MPPC), also known as the "Trust," is established. Eleven leading film companies are granted licenses to use equipment authorized by the Trust. Those companies not part of the Trust are operating illegally.

February 23. J.A.D. McCurdy makes the first manned flight in the British Empire in a heavier-than-air machine, the Silver Dart, at Baddeck, Nova Scotia, Canada.

Mary and Her Times	Canada and the World
1910 A select group from the Biograph studio spends the winter filming in California. December. Mary leaves Biograph and signs with the Independent Motion Picture Company (IMP), where she's touted as "America's Greatest Film Star."	**1910** Carl Laemmle sets up his Independent Motion Picture Company (IMP) to counteract the Trust. IMP begins a massive publicity campaign to promote its Canadian-born star, actress Florence Lawrence.
1911 January 7. Mary elopes with fellow actor Owen Moore. They keep their marriage a secret for weeks. After making thirty-five pictures, Mary leaves IMP for Majestic, where she makes five movies.	**1911** American fan magazine *Motion Picture Story* debuts. Credits begin to appear at the beginning of motion pictures, unlike today, where they appear at the end.
1912 Mary returns briefly to Biograph. Her final picture with the company, *The New York Hat*, is released December 5.	**1912** Laemmle's IMP merges with other independent motion picture companies to become Universal Pictures. Adolph Zukor founds an independent film studio and names it Famous Players. Canadian-born Mack Sennett leaves Biograph and forms Keystone Film Company and Studio in Los Angeles.

Mary and Her Times	*Canada and the World*
	William Fox establishes the Fox Film Foundation.
	April. The "unsinkable" *Titanic* sinks in the mid-Atlantic after hitting an iceberg on her maiden voyage, resulting in the loss of 1,500 lives.
1913 January 8. *A Good Little Devil* opens on Broadway, with Mary Pickford in her triumphant return to the stage. Mary signs with Adolph Zukor's Famous Players. They release *In the Bishop's Carriage* and *Caprice*.	**1913** Nickelodeons disappear with the rise of movie "palaces," showing longer films with bigger stars. The movie industry gains respect in the eyes of middle-class audiences. Hollywood replaces the East Coast as the centre of the movie-making industry.
1914 February. *Hearts Adrift*, Famous Players' first West Coast production, is released. Mary's name appears in lights on the Broadway theatre's marquee for the first time. November 14. After the success of *Tess of the Storm Country*, Zukor raises Mary's salary to $2,000 per week. Mary makes seven feature-length films this year.	**1914** August 4. The First World War begins. Britain declares war on Germany, and Canada commits 25,000 troops. Charlie Chaplin joins Keystone Studio, becoming its most important discovery. Paramount Pictures is founded to distribute the films of Jesse Lasky and Famous Players. It becomes the first successful nationwide distributor.

Mary and Her Times	*Canada and the World*
Universal (formerly IMP) re-releases thirty-three of Mary's old IMP films.	
1915	**1915**
Mary makes eight features for Famous Players.	April 22. Canadian troops at the Second Battle of Ypres, Belgium, hold their ground
November. Mary officially meets Douglas Fairbanks Sr. for the first time.	against history's first major gas attack.
	May 7. Torpedoed by a German submarine, the British liner *Lusitania* sinks off the coast of Ireland, resulting in the loss of 1,198 lives.
	California-based Triangle Films Corporation is founded by Thomas Ince, Mack Sennett, and D. W. Griffith.
	3-D film is demonstrated for the first time at the Astor Theatre in New York City.
1916	**1916**
June 24. The Mary Pickford Film Corporation is established within Famous Players, allowing Mary to produce her own films. She becomes the highest paid woman in the world.	Jesse L. Lasky Feature Play Company merges with Famous Players to form the largest motion picture company in the world — Famous Players-Lasky.
The top three film stars in America are Mary Pickford, Charlie Chaplin, and Douglas Fairbanks.	The Canadian Parliament buildings in Ottawa are destroyed by fire.

Mary and Her Times	*Canada and the World*

Mary stars in *The Pride of the Clan*, directed by French director, Maurice Tourneau.

Mary Pickford signs Hollywood's first $1 million contract with Zukor at Paramount.

1917
March. Mary stars in *The Poor Little Rich Girl*, and for the first time she plays a child throughout an entire film.

Mary goes to California, where she will make two pictures directed by Cecil B. DeMille.

Woman's Home Companion names Mary Pickford "The Ideal American Woman."

1917
April 6. The U.S. enters the war against Germany.

April 9–12. Canadians capture Vimy Ridge, near Arras, France.

December 6. A French munitions ship explodes in Halifax harbour, killing 1,630 and devastating two square miles in the working-class district of Halifax.

November 11. Armistice is declared, ending the war.

1918
April. Mary, Douglas Fairbanks, and Charlie Chaplin support the U.S. war effort by going on tour to promote and sell Liberty Bonds.

July 21. Mary stars in *Stella Maris*, playing two different characters and giving one of her best dramatic performances.

Mary leaves Famous Players-Lasky and signs with First National.

1918
Canadian women from Ontario to British Columbia win the right to vote in federal elections.

A worldwide epidemic of Spanish influenza kills 20 million people, including 50,000 Canadians.

Mary and Her Times	*Canada and the World*
November. Mary and her mother, Charlotte, set up the Mary Pickford Company. Mary now has total control of every stage of her films.	

1919	**1919**
April 17. Mary Pickford, Douglas Fairbanks, Charlie Chaplin, D. W. Griffith, and William S. Hart form United Artists, a company that will enable them to produce and distribute their own films.	May 15. The Winnipeg General Strike begins. It will last seven weeks. June 14. The first successful transatlantic flight leaves St. John's, Nfld.

1920	**1920**
January 21. Mary stars in her first picture for United Artists, *Pollyanna*. March 21. Mary Pickford and Owen Moore divorce. March 28. Mary marries Douglas Fairbanks, and the world acknowledges the popular couple as Hollywood royalty.	Douglas Fairbanks stars in *The Mark of Zorro*, his first picture for United Artists. Previously a star of comedies and westerns, Fairbanks will establish himself, with this picture, as a swashbuckling hero. In Hollywood, Lee de Forest invents the Phonofilm, the first sound-on-film process that quickly replaces sound-on-disc technology.

1921	**1921**
Mary stars in *Suds, The Love Light, Through the Back Door*, and *Little Lord Fauntleroy*, a film in which she plays dual roles. Mary establishes the Motion Picture Relief Fund (MPRF) to raise funds for needy actors.	Agnes MacPhail becomes the first woman in Canada to be elected to the House of Commons. This is the first election in which women in Canada have the right to vote. Adolph Hitler becomes the head of the Nazi Party in Germany.

Mary and Her Times	*Canada and the World*
October 21. Mary and Douglas Fairbanks begin a European tour.	
1922 Mary and Douglas buy a studio in Hollywood, naming it the Pickford-Fairbanks Studio.	**1922** Rin Tin Tin, a German Shepherd dog, becomes Hollywood's first canine movie star.
November 12. Mary's highly successful remake of her 1914 film, *Tess of the Storm Country*, is released.	The Union of Soviet Socialist Republics (USSR) is formed.
1923 September 3. *Rosita* premiers at New York's Lyric Theatre. The picture is a collaboration between Mary and German director Ernst Lubitsch.	**1923** Dr. Frederick Banting, Dr. Charles Best, and their research team, of the University of Toronto, win the Noble Prize for isolating insulin as a treatment for diabetes.
	Warner Bros. is founded and becomes one of the first large film studios in America.
1924 March. Mary's film *Dorothy Vernon of Haddon Hall* is released.	**1924** Theatres in the U.S. show double features for the first time.
Mary and Douglas sail on the *Olympic* for another European tour.	
1925 During the filming of *Little Annie Rooney*, released October 18, a plot to kidnap Mary is	**1925** Western Electric and Warner Bros. set out to develop a system to make movies with sound.

Mary and Her Times	Canada and the World

uncovered. The plotters are apprehended before they are able to carry out their plans.

1926
Mary releases *Sparrows*, her only Gothic melodrama and a stunning performance.

Mary and Douglas set sail on another world tour, but it is cut short when Charlotte, Mary's mother, becomes gravely ill.

1926
Warner Bros. releases *Don Juan*, the first Vitaphone sound film, featuring sound effects and music, although no dialogue.

Movietone, developed by Fox Film Corporation, places a sound track on the actual film, next to the picture frames, rather than on a synchronized disc.

1927
May. Mary and Douglas helped found the Academy of Motion Picture Arts and Sciences.

October 31. Mary stars with her future husband, Charles "Buddy" Rogers, in *My Best Girl*.

1927
Joseph Stalin becomes the leader of the Soviet Union.

July 1. To celebrate Canada's sixtieth birthday, the first coast-to-coast radio broadcast is made.

The era of silent films ends with Warner Bros.'s *The Jazz Singer*, starring Al Jolson.

January 9. Montreal's Laurier Palace Theatre burns, killing seventy-eight children. Thereafter, children under the age of sixteen in Quebec are banned from commercial cinemas. The ban remains in effect until the Quiet Revolution of the 1960s and the secularization of society.

Mary and Her Times	*Canada and the World*

1928

March 21. Charlotte Pickford succumbs to cancer.

June 21. Mary has her long curls cut off. Now she will be ready to take on more sophisticated roles.

1929

April 12. Mary, playing a wealthy young Southern flirt, stars in *Coquette*, her first talkie.

October 26. *The Taming of the Shrew* opens, starring Mary Pickford and Douglas Fairbanks together on the screen for the first time.

1930

Mary wins the Academy Award for Best Actress for *Coquette*, the first Academy Award given to an actress in a talkie.

1931

March 14. *Kiki* is released. Mary calls it the worst picture of her career, and it is the first Pickford picture ever to lose money for United Artists.

1928

Alexander Fleming, Scottish biologist, discovers the antibiotic penicillin.

Paramount becomes the first studio to announce that it will produce only talkies.

1929

October 19. The New York Stock Market crashes. By Thursday, October 24, the boom period of the 1920s will end. As wheat prices in the prairie provinces collapse, the Canadian economy starts to spiral downward.

In Rochester, NY, George Eastman demonstrates the first Technicolour movie.

1930

Cairine Wilson is appointed Canada's first senator.

1931

The Statute of Westminster is passed by British parliament, establishing complete legislative equality between the parliaments in Britain and Canada.

American inventor Thomas A. Edison dies at the age of

Mary and Her Times	Canada and the World
	eighty-four. One of the pioneers of filmmaking, he established the world's first film production studio, dubbed "The Black Maria," in 1893.
1933	**1933**
January 3. Jack Pickford dies at the age of thirty-three after years of alcohol abuse.	RKO's classic picture, *King Kong*, starring Canadian-born actress Fay Wray, premiers in New York City. The action-packed adventure movie smashes all previous box-office records.
March 15. Mary stars in the melodramatic movie, *Secrets*, with British actor Leslie Howard. It is reported to be the best of Mary's talkies.	
	Canadian government statistics report that twenty-three percent of Canadians are out of work.
July 3. Headlines in the *New York Daily News* read, "Doug and Mary Part."	
December 8. Mary petitions for divorce.	
December 22. Mary stars in the comedy play, *The Church Mouse*, on Broadway, then begins touring with the production on the east coast.	
1934	**1934**
April. Douglas Fairbanks is named in Lord Ashley-Cooper's divorce petition.	The Dionne quintuplets are born in Callander, ON, attracting international media attention.
Mary visits Toronto with *The Church Mouse*.	Warner Bros. becomes the first studio to shut down its

Mary and Her Times	*Canada and the World*
The Mary Pickford Stock Radio Company, Mary's own radio theatre, is launched.	distribution office in Germany as a protest against Nazi anti-semitic policies.
Mary writes her inspirational book *Why Not Try God?*	
1935	**1935**
Mary appears in Seattle in the stage version of *Coquette*.	One thousand unemployed men from Canada's prairie provinces ride the rails to Ottawa, intend-
Mary's second self-help book-let, *My Rendezvous with Life*, is published.	ing to confront Prime Minister Bennett over the 20 cents-a-day relief camps.
	Twentieth Century Pictures and the Fox Film Corporation merge to form Twentieth Century-Fox.
1936	**1936**
Mary begins her latest radio show, *Parties at Pickfair*.	December. King Edward VIII abdicates in order to marry divorced American Wallis
January 10. The divorce between Douglas Fairbanks and Mary Pickford becomes final.	Simpson. He hands the British throne to his younger brother, Albert, who becomes King George VI.
March 7. Douglas Fairbanks marries Lady Sylvia Ashley.	
December 9. Lottie Pickford dies suddenly of a heart attack.	
Mary and Jesse Lasky form Pickford-Lasky Productions.	

Mary and Her Times	*Canada and the World*
1937	**1937**
June 24. Mary marries Charles "Buddy" Rogers.	Japan invades China, beginning the Second World War in the Far East.
Pickford-Lasky Productions folds.	
1938	**1938**
Mary and Buddy launch Mary Pickford Cosmetics Inc.	American president Franklin Delano Roosevelt becomes the first U.S. president to
Mary interviews celebrities for a series of articles for the *New York Journal.*	visit Canada when he meets Prime Minister William Lyon MacKenzie King in Kingston.
1939	**1939**
June. Owen Moore, Mary's first husband, dies.	May 2. In Canada, the National Film Board (NFB) is created by the National Film Act.
December 12. Douglas Fairbanks Sr. dies.	September 10. Canada declares war on Germany, one week behind Britain and France.
	The British Commonwealth Air Training Plan is established between Canada, the U.K., Australia, and New Zealand.
1941	**1941**
The Motion Picture Relief Fund finances the building of the Motion Picture Country House in Woodland Hills, CA.	December 7. Japan attacks the U.S. Naval Base at Pearl Harbour, bringing the U.S. into the war. Canada and Britain declare war on Japan.
	In Canada, the Canadian Broadcasting Corporation (CBC) launches its news service.

Mary and Her Times	*Canada and the World*
1943	**1943**
Mary and Buddy adopt two children: Ronald, aged six, and Roxanne, aged five months.	July 4. The 1st Division of the Canadian military takes part in the invasion of Sicily.
Mary attends the opening of the Mary Pickford Bungalow in Toronto, a house she had built in support of several war charities.	British actor Leslie Howard, who co-starred with Mary Pickford in *Secrets*, dies when the DC3 he was in is shot down over the Bay of Biscayne by German fighter planes.
1948	**1948**
January 13. Ottawa premiere of *Sleep My Love*, produced by Mary, Buddy, and Ralph Cohn (Comet Productions).	Louis St. Laurent succeeds MacKenzie King as prime minister of Canada.
December 24. D. W. Griffith dies of a cerebral hemorrhage at age seventy-three.	
Mary and Buddy turn the first sod for the construction of the Mary Pickford Building at the Los Angeles Jewish Home for the Aging.	
1949	**1949**
Mary, Buddy, and Malcolm Boyd found Pickford-Rogers-Boyd (PRB), a radio and television production company in New York.	Newfoundland and Labrador enter the dominion of Canada as the tenth province.
	Canada and eleven other countries form the North Atlantic Treaty Organization (NATO), a political and military alliance.

Mary and Her Times	Canada and the World

1955
Mary's autobiography, *Sunshine and Shadow*, is published.

1955
Canada's first subway opens in Toronto.

The first Festival of Film Arts is held at the George Eastman House in Rochester, NY, to honour those who contributed the most to the silent era, 1915–1925. Mary is awarded the first "George" award.

Hockey fans in Montreal riot when Maurice "The Rocket" Richard is suspended by the National Hockey League.

1956
Mary sells her shares in United Artists, ending her relationship with the company she helped found.

1956
The United Nations General Assembly accepts Canadian Lester B. Pearson's plan for an international peacekeeping force to end hostilities in the Suez crisis.

1961
Mary is the Beverly Hills delegate to the inaugural White House Conference on Aging.

1961
Soviet astronaut Yuri A. Gagarin becomes the first human in space and the first human to orbit the earth.

1963
Mary pays her last visit to Toronto, where she appears on the television show *Front Page Challenge*.

1963
U.S. President John F. Kennedy is assassinated in Dallas, Texas.

1965
October. Mary attends a retrospective of fifty of her films in Paris, presented by the Cinémathèque Française.

1965
February 15. Canada's new maple leaf flag is unveiled on Parliament Hill.

Mary and Her Times	*Canada and the World*
1971 In Los Angeles, there is a worldwide celebration of Mary Pickford's films.	**1971** In Canada the federal government officially adopts a policy of multiculturalism.
1973 May 27. A plaque honouring Mary Pickford is unveiled near the site of her birthplace in Toronto.	**1973** In Canada the Royal Canadian Mounted Police (RCMP) celebrates 100 years of service.
1976 Mary is awarded an Honorary Oscar by the Academy of Motion Picture Arts and Sciences for her lifetime achievement.	**1976** Rene Levesque and the Parti Québécois win the Quebec provincial election.
1979 May 25. Mary is admitted to the Santa Monica Hospital after suffering a stroke.	**1979** In Canada the Conservatives under Joe Clark win the federal election.
May 29. Mary Pickford dies at the age of eighty-seven.	The first U.S. space station, Skylab, is launched from Cape Canaveral.

Bibliography

Articles

Card, James. "The Films of Mary Pickford." *Image: Journal of Photography of the George Eastman House*, 8, 4 (December 1959), 172–187.

"Mary Pickford." *American Cultural Leaders*. Jan 1, 2001. *eLibrary*. Accessed September 30, 2010

Pickford, Mary (1893–1979). *Encyclopedia of World Biography*. Thomson Gale, 1998. Academic One File. Gale Document number A148363417. Accessed September 22, 2010.

Tibbetts, John. "Mary Pickford Returns." *The World & I.* December 1, 1996. *eLibrary*. Accessed September 30, 2010.

Walraith, Jean. "First 'George' Award Presented to Silent Film Stars at Eastman." *Image: Journal of the George Eastman House*, 4, 9 (December 1955), 68–9.

Books

Brownlow, Kevin. *Mary Pickford Rediscovered: Rare Pictures of a Hollywood Legend*. New York: Harry N. Abrams Inc., in association with The Academy of Motion Picture Arts and Sciences, 1999.

Carey, Gary. *Doug and Mary: A Biography of Douglas Fairbanks and Mary Pickford*. New York: E. P. Dutton, 1977.

Eyman, Scott. *Mary Pickford: From Here to Hollywood*. Toronto: Harper Collins, 1990.

Felder, Deborah. *The 100 Most Influential Women of All Time: A Ranking Past and Present*. New York: A Citadel Press Book, 1996.

Foster, Charles. *Stardust and Shadows: Canadians in Early Hollywood*. Toronto: Dundurn Press, 2000.

Leavey, Peggy Dymond. *The Movie Years: A Nostalgic Remembrance of Canada's Film-making Capital, Trenton, Ontario, 1917–1934*. Belleville, Ontario: Mika Publishing, 1989.

Morton, Desmond. *A Short History of Canada*. Edmonton: Hurtig Publishing, 1983.

Pickford, Mary. *Sunshine and Shadow*. New York: Doubleday and Company Inc., 1955.

Reid, Phyllis J., and Bernard L. Witlieb. *The Book of Women's Firsts: Breakthrough Achievements of Almost 1000 American Women*. New York: Random House, 1992.

Wagenknecht, Edward. *The Movies in the Age of Innocence.* Norman, Oklahoma: University of Oklahoma Press, 1962.

Whitfield, Eileen. *Pickford: The Woman Who Made Hollywood.* Toronto: Macfarlane, Walter & Ross, 1997.

Windler, Robert. *Sweetheart: The Story of Mary Pickford.* New York: Praeger Publications, 1974.

Films
National Film Board of Canada. NFB Images. Shot ID: 15401 1948.

Williams, Sue. PBS Documentary. *American Experience: Mary Pickford.* 2005.

Neely, Hugh M., dir. *Mary Pickford: A Life on Film.* Timeline Films. 1997.

Radio Programs
CBC Radio News Special. "Mary Pickford born in Toronto." With Tony Thomas. May 25, 1959. The CBC Digital Archive.

Websites
Doyle, Jack. "Talkie Terror, 1928–1930." *PopHistoryDig.com*, October 19, 2010. Photoplay Magazine History.

Neeley, Hugh. *"Mary Pickford, Filmmaker." www.marypickford. com/library/about-mary-pickford.* Mary Pickford Institute for Film Education.

Index